Ezra
Nehemiah
Esther

Through the Bible with
Lance Lambert

Ezra
Nehemiah
Esther

Through the Bible with

Lance Lambert

LANCE LAMBERT MINISTRIES

Richmond, Virginia, USA

ISBN: 978-1-68389-110-9

www.lancelambert.org

Contents

Introduction

Lance Lambert, while at Halford House in Richmond, Surrey, taught a series of Bible studies in the 1960's. The audio for these messages was recorded and preserved over the years. Lance also reviewed some of his study guides from those studies and updated them later in life to be a further resource.

In the *Through the Bible* series these studies are kept as close to the original text as possible with only minor edits for clarity. Ezra to Esther is a volume published in this series which includes Lance's very helpful tools on "How to Study the Bible." Look for other volumes soon to come!

1.
Ezra—The First Return under Zerubbabel

We are going to look together at the book of Ezra. The key to this twofold book of Ezra and Nehemiah is the same as to Chronicles. That is, the house of God, the temple, is the heart of Ezra and Nehemiah. However, we find that a new note is struck and this new note is really the key to Ezra and Nehemiah. This new note is *recovery*. Wherever you turn in these two books you will find recovery. Everywhere, on every side, you will find that something is being restored, something is being rebuilt, something is being reinstituted or recovered.

The Lord's Recovery Work

The whole book breathes recovery. It is a wonderful thing to see the character of God displayed in Ezra and Nehemiah and it may be of real help to understand God's character as displayed in these two books. It is simply that the Lord is always loath to give up on anyone. This may help some of you. The Lord is loath to give up on anyone. This question of Hell, damnation, and judgment and so on is not such a facile and easy thing as some people imagine. I believe the Lord loathes the giving up of anyone for anything like that. Ezra and Nehemiah are the most wonderful examples and illustrations of the patience, the long-suffering, and the faithfulness of God. He will not let go. It reminds one of the Word of the Lord to Jeremiah, when he took him down to the potter's house, showed him a vessel, showed how it was ruined, showed how it was smashed, and then showed him how it was remade. This is just the character of our God. It is a most wonderful thing. God will not let go of anything until it is literally impossible to do anything with it.

Of course, humanity is a picture of that in general. Many of us ask the question, "Why didn't the Lord give up on humanity at the beginning altogether and start afresh in a new way?" But no! When humanity became wrecked and ruined, the Lord would not give it up, but found a way of redeeming it, restoring it, refashioning it, and reconstituting it. Do you see?

Israel is the same. I believe that is what Paul meant when he said, "In the end ... all Israel will be saved." God will not let it go. In the end, His idea in the spiritual Israel of God, will be wholly and completely realised. Now, I say that for one very, very important reason. There is this modern (and not so modern in some ways) teaching, and perhaps more than a teaching—an idea, a current notion —amongst the Lord's people that the Lord has given up what he originally had in the New Testament. That is, the church is split into so many factions, into so many smithereens, has become so corrupt, has become so worldly, so organised that, really, it is now a question of individuals finding their way to the Lord. But the Lord never lets go of what is His real thought. Ezra and Nehemiah are the wonderful examples of that.

Do you know that the Lord never rejects anything? Rather than reject something, He will deliberately stumble one of His children, put them in the far country, and purge them in the far country of every single thing that was antagonistic, and rebellious, and unyielding. Then He will bring them back, but He will not let them go. I believe that is what the Lord Jesus meant in the parable of the prodigal son. You see? The father helped the son to go. He never counselled him not to go. He never stood in his way. He willingly gave him the money to live in immorality and licence. The father gave the prodigal son the money to live in the far country and have a riotous time. Now, this is God. He would prefer to allow the whole Jewish Nation to go into exile and into captivity and to be satiated with idolatry in order to purge them, purify them, and bring them back as a nation that is now and has been ever since purged and purified from idolatry.

I wanted just to say that I feel it is something of which we have got to take note. The Lord refuses to reject anything until it is absolutely impossible. Now, that should be a great comfort to all of us. He refuses to reject anything. He may deliberately put us (if we will not yield) in the far country and allow us to have our time to the full. But the whole purpose of the Lord is to restore and to recover what has really been sought. We see this in these wonderful books of Ezra and Nehemiah.

The outline of Ezra and Nehemiah is really under one great title. It is really the last part of Chronicles: the recovery of the house of God and the bringing in of the Christ of God. That is *the* title. Under that we find three subdivisions, and I have put them under the first return under Zerubbabel, the second return (something like 50 years later) under Ezra, and then the third return under Nehemiah. Then we shall find that there are some subdivisions under that but those are the three subdivisions of Ezra and Nehemiah. They went into exile in three stages. They came back to the land and to the heart of God in three clearly defined stages.

Now, let us take the first of these stages. We will find this first stage in the first six chapters of Ezra—chapters which are absolutely vital to the rest of the book. We shall not need to spend so much time on the rest of Ezra as on these six chapters. They lay the foundation. In these six chapters, we have the first great return under Zerubbabel.

What do we find in these chapters? Ezra and Nehemiah, coming at the very end of the Old Testament age, crystallise and embody principles of recovery and principles which are basic to bringing the Lord Jesus back to this earth. So we shall expect to find principles of recovery here in Ezra.

The First Principle of Recovery

In Ezra chapter one, we come to the first principle of recovery. I expect you will all sigh when you find that the first principle of recovery is clearly a matter of *ground*. You will see that chapter one has two main things about it. The first thing is the decree of Cyrus, that is, the great proclamation in which the declaration was made for allowing the people to return and rebuild the house of God in Jerusalem. The second thing is the actual return. It is a very, very simple account indeed. There are not many verses, only eleven verses in this first chapter.

The Decree

Why do we say we find here this question of ground? Well, you and I have got to remember that this was written when the Jews were back in Jerusalem and back in the land. Now, when you remember that, you will understand how very remarkable this is. Now look at verse 2: "He hath charged me to build Him a house in Jerusalem ... God of heaven, the Lord, the God of heaven hath charged me to build Him a house in Jerusalem."

> "Let him go up to Jerusalem ... and build the House of [the Lord], the God of Israel ... which is in Jerusalem." Ezra 1:3b

> "for the House of God which is in Jerusalem." Ezra 1:4b

> "even all whose spirit God had stirred to go up to build the house of Jehovah which is in Jerusalem." Ezra 1:5b

And then, in verse 11 you will find, "All these did Sheshbazzar bring up, when they of the captivity were brought up from Babylon unto Jerusalem."

Even more remarkable, back in verse 3, the literal translation of the last part of verse 3 is this: "... the God of Israel (he is God), who is in Jerusalem."

He is God who is in Jerusalem. A remarkable statement that has given a lot of trouble to translators. You will find that nearly all the versions of the Bible differ on this verse because they are not quite clear as to what it means. Was it a reference by Cyrus as if he was thinking that this was one of the many gods and was the god in Jerusalem? But then we know that Cyrus did not believe in many gods. He believed in one God and he was the God who is in Jerusalem.

> "Some of the heads of fathers' households when they came to the house of the Lord which is in Jerusalem." (Ezra 2:68)

It is a strange thing to write, isn't it when they are all already in Jerusalem? This was written after they had come. It notes, "… which is in Jerusalem." Then if you look at Ezra 3:1, "… the people gathered themselves together as one man to Jerusalem." Verse eight says, "Now in the second year of their coming unto the house of God at Jerusalem …" It is all most remarkable because these references are about coming to the house of God when the house of God had not even been erected. In that sentence we have just read, the foundation was just about to be laid. In Ezra 6:12, again, this is the word of Darius, "… this house of God which is at Jerusalem."

It is a strange thing to write, isn't it, when they are all already in Jerusalem? This was written after they had come. It notes, "… which is in Jerusalem." Then if you look at Ezra 3:1, "… the people gathered themselves together as one man to Jerusalem." Verse eight says, "Now in the second year of their coming unto the house of God at Jerusalem …" It is all most remarkable because these references are about coming to the house of God when the house of God had not even been erected. In that sentence we have just read, the foundation was just about to be laid. And chapter

6:12, again, this is the word of Darius, "… this house of God which is at Jerusalem."

The Return

You will also notice that it is not only the decree, but the return is to Jerusalem. It does not say here in the first chapter that they returned anywhere else. In the second chapter, it tells us that they return to Jerusalem and Judah. However, in the first chapter what is clearly stated is that they all go back to Jerusalem. They come up to Jerusalem, they are brought up there.

So we find God's house can only be built on certain ground, which He has clearly defined, and nowhere else. It is a most solemn thing to try to build the house of God on any other ground than the ground which God has originally defined. It is incumbent upon us if we are going to have any part whatsoever in the recovery of the testimony of Jesus in these last days that we realise the purpose of God and understand what this question of ground means and how it works out in practice. It is absolutely essential. It is the first principle of recovery.

To be absolutely blunt and candid, the whole point is this: today you will find churches, as they are called, built on all kinds of ground. They are branches of denominations, they are on national ground, or they are on some form of teaching—either on a method of baptism or a method of church government or some certain aspect of holiness and so on. Some of them are built on pure evangelism only. They are an evangelistic agency, as if that is sufficient ground to really build and start a church. Do you see what I mean? The whole point is it is in complete chaos.

Today, if you were to go out into evangelical circles or amongst the Lord's people and ask them clearly to tell you: "On what ground can the house of God be built?" You would get the most surprising answers, from all kinds of answers to the most spiritual. The most spiritual answer would be: "on Christ." They would tell you, "You must build on what Christ did," and we would all agree. You must build on what Christ did. However, the point is, has God defined practically for us any way in the Word, any ground upon which the church is developed? We all know that the church is inherent in the life of Christ. If we allow the life of Christ to flow, the church is the result. But why doesn't the life of Christ flow in so many places? When you get devoted saints, dear saints, knowledgeable saints, praying saints, holy saints, why don't you get the church in expression? Because there is a question of ground. When we see this question of ground, then we can understand the church. The New Testament is full of this question of church ground. On no other ground can you build the house of God or initiate any work of God. It is the only ground on which you can build anything.

Now, if that were understood, overnight it would sweep Richmond clean of all kinds of things. All kinds of things would be gone. All kinds of organisations would all get back into perspective. They would all get pushed out or pushed in, but somehow or other, like a jigsaw, they would begin to get put into their different places. Then you would find there would be no Baptists and no Methodists, no Congregationalists, no Open Brethren, or anything that would be exclusive. They would just be the people of God on the ground of Christ in Richmond, and the people of God on the ground of Christ in Twickenham, and so on. There would be nothing else, no more, no less than that. Overnight, a revolution would have taken place which would change the face of the people of God. That is the first principle in recovery.

You see, our dear brothers and sisters, who are so spiritual, often overlook the most pointedly apparent thing of all because it is geographical. Some people do not believe that anything that you can hold, anything that you can see, can possibly be spiritual. But God has linked flesh and blood with spirit. This is a principle with God. Even the church down here on Earth, in its practical expression, is linked with locality. It is linked with something tangible, with something expressible. So this is the first thing to note and, my! what it would do if we all understood! What it would do to Christian workers! What it would do over this country! What it would do for the mission field if this simple principle were understood! It is the first principle of recovery. You must have this ground.

So you see, it is no good trying to build the house of God in Babylon. Many of the Jews remained, but do you know what they did? They built synagogues everywhere and they tried to make their little synagogues the temple. In Babylon, and in all other cities in Asia Minor, these little colonies of Jewry began to somehow try and reproduce the temple in some way or other. But, of course, it could only ever be a centre for teaching. It could not be anything else. The temple was in Jerusalem. God had clearly stated that there He would dwell and there He would meet His people. It is a solemn fact that this is linked with the coming of the Lord Jesus. This question of first getting the ground in Jerusalem clear, and going back to it is linked with the coming of the Lord Jesus. Similarly, the question of the church built and expressed on the right ground is linked with the return of our Lord Jesus Christ.

The Register of the Remnant

The second principle we find in this book is in chapter two. It is very simply a register of all who returned. This is the register of the first company, not for all who returned completely, but the first company that returned—approximately some 50,000 souls. Do you know this register even includes the livestock? So particular is God about what returns that He includes everything here. Here is a register that covers comprehensively the whole of the first company that returned under Zerubbabel.

Now, we must remember, if we are going to understand this at all, that the great majority remained in exile. They were respectable, they were prosperous, they were little colonies of Jewry in the Persian Empire, and furthermore, they were separated. These Jews had been purged of a tremendous amount by the captivity. They had been purified. Although they would not leave their exiled condition, yet they were purged of idolatry, and they were purged, for the most part, of intermarriage. They became tight little circles of Jewry, which would remain right down to the days of our Lord Jesus and onwards. They were called the Jews of the dispersion. They were more liberal than the Jews of the whole land but they were nevertheless, little groups—colonies—of Jews refusing intermarriage, refusing to have anything to do with the customs around them, while still making their living out of the Gentiles, having the commercial side of things in their hand wherever they were.

So you see, when we understand it, it begins to throw everything back into a proper perspective. For this first group of 50,000 that returned, it was a tremendous thing for them to leave the diaspora. It was a tremendous thing. It just simply meant that they were completely turning their back on prosperity, on ease, on a certain amount of satisfaction and rest because all persecution had long since vanished. The Jews in exile were now looked upon by the Persians as ... well ... it was good to be a Jew. It was good to be a Jew. They were looked upon as nearer to the Persians in feeling than any of the other deported races. So it was a tremendous thing for this group, this company, this remnant to leave. I want you to mark this as a principle of recovery: in recovery, it is always a remnant. You will not find anywhere in the Word of God, in any recovery of God, that it is anything but a remnant. That seems to be a principle. God always begins with all, but when it is purged and purified, when He recovers and restores it, it is always a remnant of the original.

Now, I want you to understand this very, very clearly. We must not despise the Jews that were left; they learned a lot as well. Now they came back to reading the Word of God. Ezekiel taught them that and so did Ezra. They came back to reading and studying the Word of God. Now they understood something of their history. Now they were separated for the first time fully, inwardly as well as outwardly and now they refused to bow to an idol. However, they would not, would not leave their exiled condition.

You know, this has a tremendous application for today. This is just the state of things we find today. The house of God is in ruin. The people of God are in exile spiritually. They are far away from what God really intends and what He wants. They are all trying to build the house of God in exile and, of course, that will not work. They cannot understand why the Lord does not come in and do something quickly. But it will not work. It just will not work. The Lord will not commit Himself to it, He will not undertake for it. Personally, yes, He will provide personally, but not corporately, not collectively.

What really is this? Why is this? Well, you and I have got to understand this principle of recovery: that it is always a remnant that returns. The majority of the Lord's people will not face this question of the church fully (and make no mistake about it) because of the price involved. This question of the corporate, this question of the recovering of something wrong, demands everything within us. Everything. It demands that all that we are be utterly broken and all that is of Christ be utterly devoted to Him, that is, its price is absolutely all-inclusive. There is no half measure. I believe that is the reason why you will find thousands of the Lord's people are far happier to remain in their own traditions and backgrounds, sections and factions. They think, "Oh dear! The conflict involved. The price, the cost that is involved, the sacrifice, all the trouble."

Furthermore, you must remember that, by the fall, we have all been constituted individualists. For the church to come into expression, the individualist has to be crucified in every one of us. It has to be absolutely shattered. All of us, to some degree or another have the individualist in us. The "I," the self-sufficient

"I" will be shattered. To be saved is one thing, but the church is the practical evidence of a full salvation; no fallen human beings can live together, and become part of each other, unless they are being saved. They soon fall out. They just cannot do it. The cost is too much, far too much. It means that you are just ejected and cannot go on with it.

We have to remember that those who returned, this little remnant that returned, opened themselves to affliction, they opened themselves to conflict, and they opened themselves to difficulty. Can you imagine all of the things we are going to read about in these two books of which the folks back in exile were not aware? There they were, with their prosperous little businesses, making their living very happily and prosperously out of all the Gentiles round about them. Having a good old time in many ways. They had none of the responsibilities that these who returned had. They had none of the conflict. They had none of the affliction. They knew nothing of the poverty. They did not know anything of the labour and the toil, the blood and the sweat that was known by these folks who went back. They were very happy in exile! Very happy. No doubt, some of them even went so far as to pat on the back those that had gone back. What a good thing they were doing restoring the old homeland and so on.

In actual fact, they were having a good time whereas those few that went back, went back to a desolate land. They were like the Pilgrim fathers. We must *never* underestimate their courage and their faith. Think of them. For the most part they only had 8,000 animals and there were 50,000 of them. Most of them had to trudge for four months (that is how long it took Ezra anyway) across the desert land. They trudged, and trudged, and trudged.

Can you just imagine? They had families. They had children. It was a terrible thing for them. Many a time must they have been tempted on the way to think of those back there in exile, all in their homes and their own little vineyards and olive yards and all the rest of it, very happy with their children and everything else. It is alright for some of us to pay the cost, but we do not like it when it comes to everyone connected with us having to pay the cost as well. But here, there was a tremendous cost involved. Husbands and wives and children—whole families, old people, young people—all had to pay the cost if they are going to go back.

There was a tremendous cost, but they were precious in the eyes of the Lord and a register was compiled. Here, in Ezra 2, you have got a register of every one that went back, including the livestock, every one of them. Not one was overlooked by the Lord. They went back. They were precious in the eyes of the Lord.

A Pure Pedigree

I want you to note the vital importance of history and pedigree. That is a funny thing to say, but note the vital importance of history and pedigree. If you look at Ezra 2:59–63, you will find that some of them could not prove their pedigree. I am afraid Zerubbabel and Joshua (Jeshua) were very hard on them. They put them out of the priesthood. They were allowed to stay in the land, but they were put out of the priesthood until a high priest could stand up with the Urim and the Thummim and would be able to distinguish whether they really had a pedigree.

What does this teach us? It teaches us the vital importance of a true, spiritual history and succession when it comes to our ministry as priests. To stay in the land—gathering with God's people—does not require it. But when we serve in the temple as priests—ministering and helping God's people—we must have spiritual history and experience behind us.

You know, just because you or I may call ourselves Methodists does not mean we are spiritually in the succession of John or Charles Wesley. Just because I call myself a Quaker does not mean I am in the spiritual succession of George Fox. There is a spiritual pedigree in Church history. Oh yes, a spiritual pedigree. There is a spiritual succession. The Anglicans have built what they have called apostolic succession. There is such a thing as spiritual apostolic succession. If you have read Broadbent's *Pilgrim Church*, you will have seen this spiritual succession traced from beginning to end. It is important to see that we have a pedigree, to see that behind us there is no compromise, no error, and no fallacy. We have not become tainted with the world or compromised with the world. We have not been mixed up with the things in exiled conditions. No! We have got to be severe. Some people cannot understand us when we are severe. It is not that we want to be exclusive. It is that we are safeguarding the pedigree. It has got to be safeguarded. We are not severe on welcoming God's people to the land, but we are severe on keeping a pure ministry. On the one hand, we maintain the unity of all the people of God, but on the other hand, we have got to be careful of anything that is compromised or mixed getting into the ministry to His people. Our service as priests must be based on a spiritual history.

I often wonder as I look through these lists of these men with strange-sounding names: What were they like? Who were they? Were they prosperous? Were they poor? Why did they leave? Did God stir up their spirit? I wonder what their conditions were, what their circumstances were? Many of them, no doubt, had big problems, big difficulties, and if you got down to it, you would find that every one of them had a reason to stay back in Babylon, and a legitimate reason. However, they left. They came back to Jerusalem. There we have another wonderful thing that we want to take note of. In recovery, it is a small remnant. They will be a poor and afflicted people. Since they are in this vanguard of recovery, they will open themselves up to conflict, to difficulty, and to strange, intangible, inexplicable things that the others know nothing about.

The Altar

The next thing we find is in chapter three. In the first seven verses, we find the third principle. It is this: the first thing they rebuilt when they returned was the altar and as soon as they had rebuilt the altar, they offered sacrifices on it before even the temple was rebuilt. Now, isn't that a remarkable thing? Before ever the first stone of the foundation (of the foundation!) was laid, they had erected the altar and were offering sacrifices on it. Indeed, they kept the Feast of Tabernacles before ever the temple was there, or even the first stones were laid. What does this teach us? It teaches us that the *cross* is absolutely fundamental to recovery. It is the third great principle. The first principle is ground, the second is a remnant, and the third is the cross—the cross working practically in them all.

I want you to read a very interesting little verse in Ezra 3:3, "And they set the altar upon its base; for fear was upon them because of the peoples of the countries: and they offered burnt-offerings …" A very strange thing. Now, why do you think they put the altar on its base? Because fear was upon them because of the peoples of the other countries. Now, why do you think that? Why? I will tell you. They felt that if they gave the Lord His right, the Lord would undertake for them completely. They were not afraid of those great nations about them if they gave the Lord His right.

How do you and I give the Lord His right? By trying to have fellowship with everyone? You try it. By trying to be one with everyone? By trying to be in harmony with the company? By trying to be holy? Or prayerful? How do you give the Lord His right? You give the Lord His right by allowing the Holy Spirit to work the cross deeply into your heart and life. This is the only way the Lord gets His right. There is no other way for the Lord to get His right.

The tragedy of today is that the Lord's people have bypassed the cross and built the church. That is the tragedy. They have bypassed the cross. They have only a bit of the cross—that is, that we are saved, justified by the cross—and then they build the church and what has happened? You have got a complete mess, a complete mess everywhere. You can connect people together, you can get Christians together, but that does not mean to say you have got the church. The church is produced by the working of the cross. The church is within the life of the Lord Jesus. If you want to be part of the church you must take the cross as your portion. The cross has to do a deep and a shattering work in every one of us if there would be any recovery whatsoever. Now, before ever a stone of the foundation is laid, the cross is in its position. There can be no foundation for the church until you have got the cross.

2.
The Second Return Under Ezra—The Recovery of Character

We come to the last four chapters of Ezra. The outline of Ezra really is plain in the text. The first return under Zerubbabel is the first six chapters of Ezra. The second return under Ezra is covered from Ezra 7–10. That has to do with moral character. Then the third return under Nehemiah is of course the book of Nehemiah. Remember, if you take Chronicles, Ezra and Nehemiah together, as they were originally intended to be, we have come to the last great section of the outline of these four books (I and II Chronicles, Ezra and Nehemiah). That was the recovery of the house of God and the bringing in of the Christ of God. We have already dealt with the first return under Zerubbabel and the decree of Cyrus. Naturally, as we continue on, we shall refer to it because each return is linked with the proceeding one.

We have found that the real value of Ezra and Nehemiah is that we have here revealed by the Holy Spirit in type and in symbol principles that are basic to recovery. That is, they are principles for the end of a dispensation. As they were then, in the shadow and figure of the true, this was the recovery of something at the end of the Old Covenant, of the Old Testament age, so they speak to us at the end of this age. They reveal to us and express to us principles of recovery and principles which are basic to the return of our Lord Jesus Christ.

The Recovery of Truth in Practice

In Ezra chapter seven we come to the second return under Ezra. Of the one or two things I would like you to note, the first is this: that in the first return under Zerubbabel, we were dealing with the recovery of truth in practice. Such things, for instance, as the church ground: Jerusalem is the place. All the types reiterate it again, and again, and again: The house of God cannot be built where *you* will choose, or where *you* would like. There is a certain place, and this was all the more remarkable, because this was written after they had returned to Jerusalem. It seems a bit strange for someone in Jerusalem to keep on talking about the house of God in Jerusalem, which is in Jerusalem, the God of Israel who is in Jerusalem, He is God who is in Jerusalem, and so on.

Church Ground, the Cross, and the Foundation

We have found that the first return reveals to us principles to do with the recovery of truth in practice. That is to do with the things of God. Such things as church ground and such things as the cross as being the only means by which God can produce the church on earth. This is the only means by which He can integrate us into the church and can build us up into the Head. So, first of all, we must be on the right ground, geographically. Secondly, there's got to be a real experience of the cross. That's another truth, truth in practice. Then we found the foundation. That's another truth in practice, this question of the Lord Jesus Christ as the foundation. You have the ground, you have the cross operating, and then you have a foundation laid. When you get a company of people together on the right ground the cross starts to do its work and then there is produced a foundation. This foundation is the life and the oneness of the Lord Jesus Christ.

Once that foundation is laid by the Holy Spirit, you have got the first step in building the church. The foundation has to do with the first actual part of the building of the temple. You see? But we noticed that all these things were the recovery of truth. We also notice for instance that there was such thing as conflict, that's a recovery of truth. If we are going to be frightened by the conflict, we had better pack up now and go off to our other places where we won't have the conflict. But it's a recovery of a principle. If we are going to be in anything that isn't a vanguard of recovering something for the Lord in the light of His return, then we are going to be at the heart of a terrible and at times seemingly inexplicable battle. It's no good taking it down or stopping the work because of it.

We remember how they stopped the work because they got afraid. When at last they left and refused to stop building but went straight on whether the king said so or not then the king said it was alright. They learned a lesson about conflict. Now many of us know something about conflict. I've seen it again and again. This is just a little aside, but someone takes a step, I don't know what kind of step it might be, it might be a very practical step. For some of the sisters it might be a question to do with dress or hair. For some of the brothers it might be a question to do with the office or something else. You take just some small step in faith and immediately, in the very step you take something goes wrong with it and you immediately think, "Well surely, surely if that was right, if that was right, it wouldn't go wrong. There must be something queer here, there must be something queer." But in actual fact, it is the devil, just trying something out, to see if by conflict he can start fighting you so as to make you step very smartly back and if you could only be made to step smartly back then he will keep you there. For the rest of your life you will be smartly stepping back. There won't be any real forward movement. Every step forward you will step back again a bit later, because the devil just knows how to get at you.

So you see now that it was a question of recovery of truth in all these things under the first return. Truth, it wasn't to do with character so much, it was to do with truth. Such things that are basic. You see, I said something which may have shocked some of you previously. I think it doesn't matter how holy you are, but if you're not on the right ground, you can't be built together. It doesn't matter how simple you are if you are on the right ground there's hope for you to be built as the church. Now this is what I'm getting at. There is a sphere and there are certain truths that have got to be seen and you have got to obey before there can be any outworking whatsoever. So you can have the most godly and devout and zealous people, but if they don't see the ground on which the church is built and metered by which God produces the church and the essential elements in the church, then that little group of godly, devout people will remain for year in and year out a group of godly people. Nothing will happen. They will scratch their heads and so will we if we don't understand as to why, why, why doesn't the Lord do something? There they are but nothing ever really happens. No one ever gets saved. Never any increase or any real activity and we scratch our heads and wonder what's wrong with those people.

Well this is just evidence. I'm not even going to mention names but I could take you all over the country today and show you this working out in practice. Godly, devout people together who just cannot understand why the Lord isn't committing Himself to them? Why isn't the Lord going, why isn't the Lord doing something here? We have the Word and all the rest of it, but the whole point is there is a recovery of truth. Those truths have got to be seen and then they have got to become practical and outworking. Once you get that you get the start.

The Second Return under Ezra

Now we come to the second return under Ezra and in the second return it is altogether different. In all these four chapters you do not get a single mention of rebuilding anything. The foundation, the ground, these are not mentioned. Of course, that all belongs to the first return and later to the third return. However, now we have come to something which is absolutely essential. We have come now to the next great thing in Ezra and Nehemiah that the Holy Spirit reveals to us. It is what we would call inward spiritual character or moral character.

In the second return that is the next thing we find. Everything deals with the recovery of an inward character. Now, we must mark the order. In evangelical Christendom today, it is the recovery of an inward character first and then you build the church. But the Holy Spirit has put it the other way around. It is just because evangelical Christendom has followed what is seemingly logical and rational that it is in such a hopeless mess. If we could only get every newly born believer, the moment they are saved, to see this question of ground and see this question of the church, then we could preach and preach and preach, and minister and minister and minister, and talk and talk and talk about inward character and everything would be safe. Because all we would say would build them up into what God is doing. Otherwise, you go on and on with the other, and you end up in pure Christian individualism, which is the curse and the blight of Christianity today.

We are really at a point of tremendous importance in the Old Testament. We have come to the second great return under Ezra and now we find everything is to do with moral character. Everything in the second return is dealing with people, not dealing with things. Everything. It is all people—not wars, not firm foundations, not ground, not stones, nothing else like that anymore. It is all people, people, people. What is the people's attitude? What is the people's reaction? What is the attitude of the leaders? What is the attitude of the elders? The chief men, the rulers ... what are their attitudes? What are their reactions to the law? What is Ezra's reaction? What is his attitude? The whole of this part, these four chapters are to do with the inward character which gives rise to an attitude and to reaction.

Now that is very true. You betray your character and I betray my character by my attitude to situations and by my reaction to things. Very quickly we react, and we cannot help ourselves. If only we knew it, we are betraying a character. It is amazing for instance, how some people will take suffering. We all say sometimes, even of a person of the world, they have got character. Other people just go to pieces. They are just absolutely hopeless; you cannot do anything with them. Their legs, arms, head—they are all over the place. You have to spend your time sort of bringing them together somehow, and it is a wearying business. Other people, they just react in the most amazing way and we say, "Well that person has got character because of the way they can take it." Do you see? Our attitude and our reactions reveal character and these four chapters are chapters of attitudes and reactions, all the way through. It is simply a question of character, moral character.

It is very interesting that in this second return the Holy Spirit focuses on one major matter. This is the heart of these four chapters. The Holy Spirit focuses upon one major matter which is mixed marriage. Of course there are other events related in these four chapters, but the main matter is this question of marriage—marriage with aliens, with those who are foreigners, outside of the people of God. Now straightway, this really reveals the heart of the matter in a sense, as we shall see. That is why the Holy Spirit attaches such a great importance and seemingly such severe measures to this whole question of mixed marriages. When we read it, I think some of us will be just a little shocked at the way Ezra uncompromisingly demanded that certain measures be taken. Many of us tend to think of the Old Testament as the Old

Testament and leave it like that, but I think if we were to wake up and think of it happening in our day, we would realise what a problem it would have created. So there are the preliminary things about these four chapters.

One other thing I would like also to point out is that between Ezra six and Ezra seven, there is a period of approximately 60 years, more or less. This period is passed over in virtual silence. In fact, as far as Ezra and Nehemiah is concerned, it is in complete silence. However, this is the period when Queen Esther reigned as queen of Persia so you have got to insert the book of Esther between Ezra chapter six and Ezra chapter seven.

The Return to Jerusalem

Now beginning with Ezra seven, we will look a little more closely at these chapters. They are divided into two: chapters seven and eight deal with the return to Jerusalem, and chapters nine and ten deal with conditions that they found on arrival at Jerusalem. First of all, we shall very briefly run over the contents of these chapters and then we will seek to draw out some of the lessons.

In chapters seven and eight we have the return to Jerusalem described. The first ten verses, Ezra 7:1–10 are literally a brief résumé that covers the whole of these four chapters. Then in Ezra 7:11, we get down to the actual return. The first thing that caused the return was the decree of King Artaxerxes to Ezra. As far as we know, it is probable that Ezra was in the government. It is very probable and is highly believed, more generally now by scholars, that Ezra occupied a very high position probably in the Jewish Affairs Department of the Persian government.

We know, for instance, that the Persian government, like the Babylonian government that preceded it, was a highly organised empire. They had not only a home office, but also a foreign affairs office and a deported peoples department. An official who had been trained in exile of the nationality of each of these deported peoples represented them and worded the decrees and laws in a way that they could understand and so on. As far as we know Ezra was probably of quite high rank in the government.

This decree of Artaxerxes, embodied in a letter, was sent to Ezra and this was the beginning of the second return. He was given freedom, a greater freedom in some ways than even Cyrus gave, not only to take anyone who wanted to go, but he was allowed to draw upon the royal treasury a remarkable sum. In actual fact it has been estimated that he took back something like one million pounds worth in silver and gold alone. Some people think, "Oh can that be true?" Now this is not so strange. We know for a fact that Alexander the Great, when he took the Persian Empire, took 14 million pounds worth of loot from the royal treasury. So it is quite feasible that Ezra did, in actual fact, take such a large sum of money back with him. It was lavish, absolutely lavish. If you read the letter of Artaxerxes, I think you will be a little bit surprised at the way in which it was worded and also the very, very generous tone and the helpful nature of it.

From that then, we go to Ezra's reaction, which is another little lovely reaction embodied in the last part of chapter seven. When we come to chapter eight we have a register which is so like Chronicles, Ezra and Nehemiah. We have a genealogy and a register of all those who returned with Ezra. We have already looked at the register of those who returned with Zerubbabel.

Now we have here a register of roughly 1,300 people, which only included men. The ladies and children are not included in this; they and their children are included in their husbands. The men are evidently, as it were, taken to be the heads of families. So in actual fact, the number is much greater than it would seem. We have something like about 1,300 men.

We also have the matter of the Levites. When Ezra comes to list everyone, he is very methodical because he is a ready scribe in the law of the Lord. When he comes down to list everything, the word used is "he ticked them off" as he went through them. Before they went down, there were no Levites there. This caused great concern with Ezra. He could not possibly leave without Levites. He must have Levites. We shall see the reason for that in a moment. So they waited for a little longer while a deputation was sent to a Levitical colony of Jewry in exile and quite a large number of Levites did at last return with them.

Then they fasted. They spent quite a few days at the river; as far as we know it was a canal somewhere near the Babylon region. There beside the canal they spent a while fasting and seeking the Lord in prayer finding out His mind, humbling themselves before Him because they had a long, arduous journey. They began in spring which would have been quite bearable, but they had four months trek across the very hot desert. Although they took the route which would avoid the worst part of the desert yet most of them would have probably had to have gone by foot and it was a pretty difficult type of journey with the possibility of marauding bands and much else on the way.

At last they started out. They took four months surviving in the heat of the mid-summer, and they took all the silver and the gold.

They weighed it before they took it and then they weighed it in Jerusalem in the house of God. Twice it was weighed: before they started out on the journey and then when they got there it was weighed in the house of God. One by one each piece was weighed and then each piece was recorded. That is also something that we must look at. So that really covers these two chapters.

The Recovery of Inward Character

What are the lessons that we can draw from this? We are speaking now of the recovery of inward character. We must understand that if we stress the question of ground and the question of the church and its absolutely vital nature to all God's purpose being the very heart of God's plan and economy, we must never forget that deeper than the recovery of truth there has got to be the recovery of an inward character. Everything finally breaks up and disintegrates because of the lack of true spiritual character. Always. It is a tremendous thing to understand the truth and to be given to the truth, to see what God is after and to see what God is doing and to give ourselves to it. However, it is another thing for the Lord to be producing a moral character, a spiritual character, a Christ-like character in us. Therefore when we come to this, we are coming to something which is essentially all to do with the character, the inward personal character. Of course you know as well as I do that everything in the end is coloured by the character of the people that constitute it. The church should be just the reproduction of the character of Christ, that's all. It should just be simply that the world should be able to touch the Lord Jesus here on earth again in His people. That is the church.

That is what we understand in the Scripture as the church—the body of our Lord Jesus. It is the Lord Jesus here on earth living again in His people in a corporate way so that men and women on earth can touch Him and know Him again. But this is a question not just of truth, even in practice. It is a question of character.

A Free Will Offering

The first thing we find about true spiritual character is something that I think is going to surprise everyone. It issues from the voluntary giving of oneself wholly to the Lord. Now let us look at Ezra 7:13, "I make a decree, that all they of the people of Israel, and their priests and the Levites, in my realm, that are minded of their own free will to go to Jerusalem, go with thee." Minded of their own free will. Then I want you to note verse 15: "To carry the silver and gold, which the king and his counselors have freely offered." This is the king and his counselors that have freely offered. Then, note again in verse 16: "And all the silver and gold that thou shalt find in all the province of Babylon, with the freewill-offering of the people, and of the priests, offering willingly for the house of their God which is in Jerusalem."

If you read through this letter and through chapter seven, there is one thing that is going to hit you. The heart of the question is that there were those who were minded to go to Jerusalem of their own free will. This is at the heart of the question of a remnant and the heart of this question of recovery. As far as spiritual character goes, it never comes from high-bound duty. If only we could understand this. There are always some of us who grit our teeth and just go through with things in a sense of duty. There is no joy about us, no peace about us, no real service about us, and no real worship about us. It is just that hard inward gritting of the teeth, and going through with it because it is the Lord's will for you—grimly, grimly. It is a question of grim death. You know, you can see the clenched jaw spiritually in some of us as we sort of jut out our chin and say, "We've got to get through this thing."

Well, there is a sense in which we need determination and steadfastness, but spiritual character never comes from such a spirit. It never comes from such a spirit, never! That is why in such people, spiritual character is lacking. It is lacking. It is not there. Spiritual character comes from a person who has got through. I know that is a hackneyed phrase amongst us, but it is from a person who's got through on the deepest level. Pardon me speaking like this, but you cannot kid me that it is really victory to grit your teeth and go through with it because it is the will of God, as if the Lord wants that kind of reaction in His people. That is not victory. Do you know what that is? It is an evidence of self. It is an unwilling self-life being dragged into the service of God, that's all. An unwilling self-life being dragged into the service of God. You and I should get with the Lord so that that self-life will be absolutely shattered so that we can then willingly give ourselves to the Lord.

Spiritual character is produced in those who have a mind, who are minded of their own free will, to go to Jerusalem. That is why it says in Nehemiah, the joy of the Lord was their strength. They had got so through that they did not give two hoots what happened to themselves. The joy of the Lord was their strength. They got through to such a place that what was joyful to the Lord was their joy.

Take for instance a Sunday morning gathering. I see so many dear saints who are trying to praise the Lord. You see, their whole point is simply this: we have to praise the Lord. It should not be like that. It is only an evidence of the self-life, that's all. It is only an evidence of the self-life. Just imagine it. I do not know what some of our parents or relatives or loved ones would think if we spoke to them like that, "Well, I have got to love you, you know, just got to." How very grieving and injurious it would be to relationships if we all went around to each other saying, "Well, I have got to, I have just got to ... I like you," through gritted teeth. You know that kind of thing. That is what we do with the Lord, you see? We speak to Him through gritted teeth all the time, not through a life that loves Him, but through a kind of, "Well, we have got to do it."

Now this is just simply because there is a self-life in the back which has never been devastated, never yet been shattered. It is there, it wants something, it wants to get somewhere, it is prepared to do it the way of the Lord certainly because it knows it is the only way. It knows that in the end it is the only way of real joy in the Lord, but it must have something for itself. Of course going this way, there is nothing for itself, therefore it moans and groans and cries. It is the fly in the ointment. Straightway we come up against this. You see this inward moral character issues from the voluntary giving of oneself.

You will note if you read through this chapter that on one side is the will of God and on the other side is the willingness of the people. All the time Artaxerxes keeps on saying, "What is the will of the Lord for you?" and "Whatsoever the Lord commands you to do, do it," and so on and all the rest of it. Next, alongside it he keeps on speaking of your free will: "... minded of your own free will."

Well, you see that is just the ticket. That is just how the Lord would have us do things. He said that he wants you to do something, but He does not want you to grit your teeth and do it grimly. He wants you to so die in that spot that you do it joyfully. You see when we cannot praise the Lord and we cannot express real worship, it is simply because what rejoices the Lord does not rejoice us. That is putting it mildly and simply. It just does not rejoice us. What the Lord finds really rewarding and delightful is something that we do not find rewarding and delightful, therefore when the Lord is amongst us singing with joy, we are there grimly. It is a question of freewill.

Some people cannot understand why we do not rebuke those with this disposition. We do not rebuke them because they are not prepared to be rebuked. It is a principle. When we know that someone is so given to the house of God, that they do not mind how you come down on them or what you say, then we do tell them. But we are not here to be dictators and hammer down on people who want to go this way or go that way or go the other way. You see, it is the whole point. It is the whole nature of this life. In this question of fellowship, everyone is free to do exactly what they want. Sometimes people get criticised because they will not do things without each other, but we do not blame anyone who does not want to do anything. If they want to do that, they can do that. If they have got the Lord's mind, God bless them. However, some of us could not do it, we have been in a way in which we cannot do that. We are bonded together in that way, you see? That's free will. It's not a dictatorship. It's not some iron-fisted thing that comes down. It began with a voluntary giving of ourselves to the Lord and to one another. It is this free will business, as we have said, that lies at the root of so much. Here is the Lord's sovereignty; here is the Lord's slavery. Here is something that is just sheer bondage to the Lord; on the other side it is something that you enter into freely of your own will.

This produces character. There is no doubt about it. You take every single person that is doing something out of high-bound duty and there is a sense of defeat about that life. It is a sense of meanness[1], a sense of poverty, a sense of narrowness. You just feel it when you touch it. But you find anyone with real spiritual worth has an enlargement about them, and you will find every time, they are people who are really serving the Lord. I mean they are not finding it easy at times, but they are serving the Lord because they have willingly given themselves and their all to the Lord. To them the whole question of all these things that worry so many of us: money and time, leisure and friendships, work and everything else, is all worldliness. Once you settle that in one fell swoop, you are something very big. Some of us I am afraid just go through each one by digit. It is much the best at the very beginning to settle the whole thing in one fell swoop and give it right over to the Lord. Henceforth, time, home, family, work, everything is the Lord's.

Utter Dependence Upon the Lord

Then you find another thing mentioned in Ezra 8:21–23: fasting. You may be very surprised, but fasting is something that issues in spiritual character. I do not care what anyone says, you will

---

1 From the idea of the older English meaning—stingy, poverty, narrowness, lack of excellence..

never find spiritual character without fasting. Of course, I do not mean just outward fasting or dieting and so on, but I mean that before they ever started on the journey back to the promised land, they fasted in order to seek the Lord diligently. Now forget the abstinence from food as a *thing* and get to the *point* of their fasting. It was to give themselves without any worrying or distractions to the Lord that they might diligently, *diligently* find His mind about the way ahead. This reveals something. It reveals a dependence upon the Lord. You see, when people are independent, they do not fast. Good gracious, no. Thousands of others have done the journey to Jerusalem I should imagine. Call them. Find out what you have got to take, what kind of weather you are going to meet on the way, what might be the possible trouble, but the king has offered a whole attachment of troops to guard you. "Ah, we should be alright. We stand as much chance of getting through to Jerusalem safely as the other caravans that go." That will be the normal person's reaction. "Oh, we must have some prayers before we go. We must ask the Lord's people to pray for us on the way, too," but that is as far as it goes. But you see here Ezra's attitude is one that reveals the most remarkable dependence upon the Lord. He has broken self-confidence and he has broken the confidence in anything else.

Do you know that Ezra refused the king's protection? He said, "No, no, no! The Lord will take care of us." So like fools, they started out on a four month journey across the desert that was just packed with marauding bands of Arabs, and they were all known to be exceedingly dangerous. But you see they were alright. They started out in utter dependence upon the Lord. They had crossed their bridges, long before they came to them, in prayer. They had been down on their knees before the Lord in fasting and they sought diligently the mind of the Lord. They humbled themselves just in case there was anything uncovered. Some people are very silly, in this question of covering. They just think that you are all right if you do not know what you are doing, but that is not so. It is not so. Consequently, they sought the Lord diligently before they took a step in case there was anything anywhere that could give ground that might mean the Lord could not protect them completely. You see? So they diligently sought the Lord.

What a wonderful thing it is, an attitude of utter dependence upon the Lord—but more than that, an attitude of utter obedience to the Lord. It was not a sham. It was not one of these prayer meetings where you just pray that the Lord's will be done but it does not matter what happens, it's already going to be done. It was not that at all. They were perfectly prepared to be flexible in the hands of the Lord and utterly obedient to the Lord.

Now that is the lordship of Christ in practice. You see, you call the Lord, Lord. What does that mean? It means that you are dependent upon Him. You are not only dependent upon Him but you will be utterly obedient to Him. It is no good you calling the Lord, Lord unless you are prepared to be dependent and prepared for the way the Lord will take you to make you dependent upon Him. He will smash all self-sufficiency and independent spirit, even of a man like Ezra, with all his learning and cultural refinement, to the point where he absolutely leans heavily and wholly upon the Lord. That is the lordship of Christ.

You see, it would have been so easy. So many other people have made the dangerous journey, why not just make it? Why all the need of fasting? What is all this need for seeking the Lord's mind? Ah, it is because these people are under the government of the Lord in a personal, direct way. They dare not take a step, not if a thousand other companies of the Lord's children go that way. They dare not take a step along that road unless they know the Lord is directing them and governing them and leading them. This produces spiritual character. Spiritual character comes from being directly under the lordship of Christ. So you see character is produced there.

The Hand of the Lord Upon Me

In Ezra 7:6, 9, and 28 there is this little phrase that Ezra uses again and again. You will notice it again in Ezra 8:22, 31 and there are one or two other instances of it too. The little phrase is: "the hand of the Lord upon me". What did he mean? Think about it. Do you know what he meant? He was speaking of the laying on of hands almost. The hand of the Lord upon me. What is this a picture of? It was the picture of the Lord, as it were, just guiding Ezra and their company. And he attributed everything to the hand of the Lord upon him. Everything in these four chapters is attributed to the hand of the Lord upon him, for good. This just means that his head was under God's hand. His hand was upon Ezra.

You see, that is the meaning of the laying on of hands in the Old Testament and the New Testament, in essence. Your head comes absolutely under His head. "The hand of the Lord is upon me." It is a practical expression of lordship. You remember that when we have to fast before the Lord and to the Lord, there is no merit in abstaining from food or anything like that.

It is a question of being utterly before the Lord in order to find the Lord's mind because we're dependent upon Him and we wish to be obedient to Him. It produces spiritual character. This is a daily thing, a daily action you can take to be leaning on the Lord. You do not have to spend your time in prayer; you can be in unceasing prayer. Prayer is dependence upon the Lord; that is all prayer is. A man who does not pray is a man who is not dependent. But a dependent person prays. They cannot help it. You get to a state where you do not even know when you are praying or when you are not praying quite frankly. You talk and talk and talk inside to the Lord referring and deferring to Him all the time. Really, quite honestly you do not know when you are praying and when you are not praying, except that when you get on your knees you do know that is prayer. But when you pray unceasingly, it is an inward communication that you cannot explain that you just are continually talking to the Lord. When you see things you just turn it to the Lord: "Lord, what do You think about that? What about that?" You cannot explain it, but there you are.

A Register of The People

Then again you find a register in chapter eight. And there are possibly about 3,000 if you would count all the wives and children and others in the company that returned with Ezra. Now what does this reveal to us? It reveals another very important point I would like to make. Moral character is personal. It is personal. The greatest danger of an understanding of the church is that we hide in the whole, in the rest. Moral character, spiritual character is personal but I want you to know, it is produced in and through a company. Always. True spiritual character is always produced in a company because it is tested there. It cannot be tested anywhere else. You get these dear people that live absolutely alone and they seem very pious and godly and good, but they have never been put to the test.

Ah, a lot of us could be godly and pious if we were all alone and did not have any irritating people around us or very nice people around us who we just collide with all the time, if we had no one to get on our nerves or all the rest of it. You know what I mean. We would be very, very nice if we had a little cottage somewhere down in the country and could spend our time reading and just looking at the lovely views far away from all those others. We would have ourselves of course to give us a lot of trouble, but most of us are so in love with ourselves we can somehow get over that problem on the whole. It is *other* people. It is other people and believe me, if you start living with other Christians or other Christians start living with you or working with you, well what you have comes down to being real ... or it goes. It always happens. Some people get awfully shocked at what they find once they get on the inside of the company of the Lord's people. They think it is really terrible. They thought that we were all so sweet or something. Just get inside and you begin to see it all comes down to the reality. Some will seem so gracious until you suddenly bump up against them and then you suddenly see that they are not so gracious, and so it goes on and all the rest of it.

This last group of people that returned was the smallest, but it was a real group of people, a company of people. Now you think about it. On that arduous journey, they had to live together, eat together, and do everything together. They had to be disciplined. This means there was a history of fellowship and of maintaining the unity. Spiritual character comes out of that. It comes out of fellowship.

Many of us get hurt through fellowship. We become disappointed in fellowship. We become disillusioned in fellowship and then we start to withdraw into our little shell. Of course, the more we withdraw into our shell, the less we get hurt; that is true. We get so far into our shell in the end that as I say, we do not get hurt that much. However, you immediately become static spiritually. You are done. That is the end. Of course there are dozens of pillars of salt amongst the people of God. People just turned away and they are done. That is all. You cannot have much fellowship with a pillar of salt. It is preserved and embalmed.

Of course, amongst the Lord's people you do get such cases of preserved and embalmed saints. We cannot put our finger on what happened, but somewhere or other in their history, they just became disappointed or disillusioned. They drew into a shell and that was the end. Naturally, we can blame everyone else, but the whole point in this question of going on with the Lord is our *selves*. I am absolutely convinced that you cannot be really effective unless there is something inside which is, as it were "affectable". Do you know what I mean? Most of us have got this something inside which reacts, and on the deeper level of fellowship together, those are the things that we have to get through on. If we do not get through, we die spiritually, and as I said the Lord's people are littered with such terrible tragedies that are all around, they are static. They just could not bear it anymore and they drew into a shell.

This spiritual character is produced, not by drawing out, but by getting through. The only way you can get through of course is dying to self. The only thing that can ever get hurt in you and me is self, nothing else. We need not try to think it is spiritual. The self is the only thing that gets hurt and if you and I would only take all the rebuffs and the disappointments and disillusionments we find in one another as a means by which the Lord will bring us into a deeper experience of the cross, we shall then go on. We shall blossom and flourish spiritually and our spiritual character will come. It is a vital factor in producing character.

Then again, and I am going to pass over this rather swiftly, you also find Levites mentioned here in chapter eight. Ezra refuses to move until there are Levites amongst them. Who do Levites speak of? They speak of those who are utterly given to the service of the Lord. Utterly. Absolutely utterly. They have no inheritance in the land, nothing. They are just wholly given to the Lord. That is interesting isn't it? Spiritual character is just that. Those whose aim and life is to the service of the Lord and His interests.

Silver Before Gold

Then I want also you to note silver and gold. When we come to this question of silver and gold in Ezra 8:24—34, we come to a most interesting thing. This silver and gold is mentioned in the first return, but it is not emphasised there. Here it is absolutely emphasised. We are not only given the whole number, which we were in the first, but we are also given the weight and much else.

Another interesting thing is that silver precedes gold in every instance in these four chapters. Now isn't that an interesting thing? I think that nearly all of us know that silver in the Bible speaks always of redemption or justification. Righteousness imputed, that is, the Lord Jesus given to us as a gift, as our righteousness before God. Now everywhere in the Bible silver speaks of righteousness like that—justification, being justified freely, as a gift of God. We cannot do anything for it. We cannot earn it. We cannot work it or anything else. It is given to us.

Wherever you find silver in the Bible, it always stands for Christ for us—redemption—Christ for us—redemption or justification. But gold never speaks of that. Gold in the Scripture always speaks of divine character or of sanctification, or let me put it another way: Christ in us. Silver speaks of righteousness imputed, but gold speaks of righteousness imparted. Now, silver precedes the gold. Isn't that interesting? Frankly, I believe this is the key to moral character. Many of us get into a mess because we so want to see ourselves changed. We want to see the Lord produced in us. We put the gold before the silver. However, the Lord would have us first absolutely rooted in the fact that Christ is our righteousness that we are in ourselves worthless. We have got to get that clear. The Lord will take great pains to show us ourselves, to make us very miserable and leave us, as it were, to stew in that misery until we come to the place that we recognise there is absolutely no righteousness in our flesh whatsoever. Then, of course, we come to the wonderful fact that the Lord never expected to find any in our flesh anyway. What I can say is that some of you will still be worrying tonight about this very thing. Until you see it, you will never get the peace that comes with it. Yet, it is part of your salvation and mine.

You see, Christ is our righteousness. Christ is our righteousness. This is silver. Now this silver was weighed and recorded. It is the basis of everything else that God does. But once that is in its place and rightly understood and laid hold of, then God starts to do the other work—to produce a righteousness in us by His Holy Spirit. As soon as we get our eyes on that, we shall be lost. We will. We have to keep our eyes on the silver. God works the gold. You keep your eyes on the silver and God will speak of the gold increasing. You must keep your eyes on the thing that is first— Christ for us. God will do the rest with Christ in us, you see? But these two things are absolutely together, absolutely together.

Spiritual character is based in Christ for us and produced by Christ in us. Remember that. You will never have any spiritual character while you are waiting for it to be in you. You must understand first that Christ is spiritual character for you. The whole point is so spiritually rational. God deals with us so severely and so devastatingly, but unless we know what it is to have the Lord Jesus as our righteousness before God, we will let go in despair, in absolute despair. We shall let go, and then we shall be lost in the blackness of darkness.

We must take hold of Christ for us, our righteousness, our acceptance with God, our salvation. Then God starts to work in us when we take hold. As soon as I get my eyes on the gold, the gold stops; as soon as I put my eyes on the silver, God starts to produce the gold. Isn't that strange? But it is absolutely true. If you keep on looking, saying, "Is there anything more of the Lord Jesus in me, I wonder? Is there anything more of the Lord

Jesus in me?" The more you look, the more miserable you become, the more despondent you become, and the work of the Holy Spirit starts to slow down until it stops. But the more you take hold of the Lord Jesus and say, "Christ is my righteousness before God", the more the Holy Spirit takes hold of the Lord Jesus in you and produces this spiritual character.

That is why when you talk with the people that you think are most like the Lord, if they were really to talk with you openly you would find they are most conscious of the vileness of themselves. It is a strange thing. I often meet people who are so like the Lord and I think that surely they must be conscious of it, it just breezes out of them. It sort of hits you as you come anywhere near them. They are really genuine. There is really something of the Lord there. They must know it; they walk in it all day. I feel it when I touch them, so they must know it. But when I speak with them they are, "Oh!?" They really have a genuine opinion of themselves which is terrible! How have they got through? It is because of Christ for them. That is their theme—Christ for us. Well, it is something we have to remember.

Mixed Marriage

The matter of the last two chapters can be more simply dealt with, because it is one matter. The last two chapters deal with this one matter of mixed marriage. This is interesting. By the way, this silver and gold is weighed and is recorded in the house of God. Just mark that will you? Everything that is of the Lord Jesus is for the house of God. It is weighed and recorded.

Now at last, in the last two chapters we find the conditions they found on arrival. Poor Ezra, when he got back, what did he find? He found a terrible state of affairs. To come back to what he thought was wonderful yet when he got there, he found the whole thing was in decay. They came to him and look at the list they gave him. It was almost funny: Perizzites, Hittites, Jebusites, Amorites, Moabites, Ammonites, Egyptians. Well, if you look back through that list, you will find you almost go right back to Abraham. You find that all the people who have ever troubled the work of God are there. Now after the captivity, after all that, some of them have turned and they are back to the old life. What have they done? They have taken wives of these very people. It is an old trouble that is all starting up again.

Well, well, well, what do we learn here? Spiritually, this is what we learn: an understanding of mixed marriage is the heart of spiritual character, because it is always the curse in God's work. I am talking spiritually now. I am not just talking about it physically; I am talking about it spiritually. It is a curse in God's work. What do we mean by mixed marriage spiritually? We mean that compromise, that mixture, whatever it is, that awful mixture that in the New Testament is called adultery. Spiritual fornication and adultery. It is that awful playing with this world, alliances with this world. You do not have to go to the movie picture, or smoke, or drink, or all the rest you know, to have alliances with this world. They can be in the prayer gathering. They can be there.

Now, why marriage? Because here, we are touching the deepest part of our beings—our affections, our feelings, our desires. It is always those deep, mysterious things in us that are unyielding when it comes to the Lord. Oh, many of us will be caught on many other things: money, time, much else, but it is those deep, deep things to do with our affections, to do with our feelings, to do with our desires, that will pound you and will not yield. You know, we will go along with the Lord. You see these people have come back. No matter their history, they had come back, and not only had they come back, but they have built the house. They are there. They wanted to go the way of the Lord. They were prepared to go a long way with the Lord. They were on the right ground, but they had brought their alliances with them. See?

Now that speaks to a lot of us. We will go a long way with the Lord, but, but, but … there are those deep, deep, deep things that we do not talk about, in which we are compromised, in which we are mixed, impure. Something that can only be described as the spirit of this world is there. Friendship with the world and until that thing is dealt with, there can be no real spiritual character. Spiritual character comes from that kind of thing being dealt with on the deepest level. That is why the Lord is giving some of us such a terrible time, because it is on that deepest level that the Lord would get us through. You know, it is no good getting us through on one level, and then leaving us on that level. He wants to get us through on the deepest level—our affections, our feelings, our desires, these deep things. We can be free. We need not go to places, we need not do certain things, we need not read certain things. But, oh, there might be all kinds of things and it is those things that give rise to jealousy and strife and backbiting and faction and backchat. It all comes usually from something that is unyielding deep down in a person and it is usually covetousness. It is something that desires, something that feels, and something that wants. Those are the things so often at the bottom of it.

No wonder dear old Nehemiah, when we come to him, we shall find, he lifted up his skirts and he chased that man out of the house of the Lord. At the last part of the Old Testament history, here is a godly man chasing another man out of the house of God. But the whole point was, Nehemiah was not even going to leave one single impure association in the house of the Lord.

Here you have got to the very heart of it. You and I can only ask ourselves a question: is there anything that corresponds to such a mixture in us? Really, deep down within us, is there such a thing that corresponds to such a mixture? Is there something that is compromised, something just somehow or other we are not through on? There, that is the thing that matters. You have got the ground, you have the foundation, you have got the people, you have the cross working, in some measure anyway, and you have got the house built; but God uses Ezra to deal with inward character.

When you read these two chapters you cannot but be impressed with this man, Ezra, this man's humility and weakness. He is not the man with the big stick, you know, wielding it. Oh, this terrible idea of authority! This terrible idea of authority that it is unapproachable, and heavy handed, and so on. How does this man react to this thing? Does he get up into the pulpit and sort of look at them with fiery eyes and so on? Well, no. His first reaction is the most strange reaction to us. Here, this dignified, refined, cultured man, holding a high position in the Persian government of all things, and what does he do? He tears his garments, he pulls out his hair, he pulls out his beard! What a disheveled sight that man must have been. Then it says he just simply went before the Lord and stayed there for a day. It is as if he is appalled. He sat down confounded. The Revised Standard Version says, "appalled." He was so overcome.

The Response

Now, this is the question I want to ask: Are you so identified with the purpose of God, and the interests of God, that when such a thing happens this is your reaction? It is simply the reaction of a humble, meek man. Might I add, any other kind of man would have battered all their heads together somehow, at least in preaching. He would have somehow or other told them all off, but this is a man who had the interest of God at heart. He is a broken man because of something in which he actually had no part whatsoever. Now, if he had a foreign wife, it would have made all the difference. You would have expected him to have sat down and wept and cried, but he had not, therefore, he was in the position where he could have gone and told the rest. However, you do not detect any of that in his prayer. His prayer is "our guilt," "our sin," "our exceeding great wickedness." It is all himself, as if he is the wickedest and vilest sinner that ever walked in the house of God.

His prayer is one of the loveliest in the Bible. It was the spirit of travail and it says he knelt, which is a very unusual thing for any Jew to do. They stood always, but he knelt. He was in such grief that he knelt before the Lord. What I want you to note, is that that man's travail was the thing that without a word being said, brought everyone together. There was no roundtable conference, no trying to put something over to the rest, really. Because of what happened inside the leadership, the immediate effect upon those that were so wrong, was that they came weeping.

Now this is the heart of spiritual character in leadership, I think. We all fall short of it, those of us with any leadership roles fall dismally short, but it is the heart of it. You do not just throw your weight around, nor do you take that sort of assertive, proud attitude that, "you cannot tell me anything." This was a spirit that was so utterly real and genuine before the Lord that he had an "in" with the Lord immediately.

This was one of the greatest days in the history of the people of God. Never before this day could they say, "We will put away our wives." It was the severest thing. That day little children were torn away from their fathers never to see them again. Wives were turned out and sent back to their own country never to see their husbands again. It was a terrible day. There were 113 wives, if I am right, in the end turned out of house, and home, and everything; with their little ones, some of them. Severe measures. Terrible measures, terrible measures. But you see again, it was free will. Ezra did not batter them into it. His attitude reacted in them; it drew out a reaction. They came and they said, "What shall we do? We are with you. You do it". Then when they said, "You do it," Ezra was firm.

Now, that is just not like us, because if someone loves us and they come to us and they say, "Look here, we have all been very wrong. We can see by what we have done to you, that we have been very wrong. We are very sorry." Well of course, usually the right thing to do is to say, "Ahh, it's alright. It's all right. Don't worry. Don't worry. Of course, there are those grieved, but I am sure the Lord will understand. I understand". No, Ezra said straightway as soon as they came to him, "No, you must put away those wives straightway. There is no way through until you have done that," and they did it.

Well, that was a terrible day, but it was the greatest day in the history of God's people. Never before had there been such willingness—not like that. That was a great day. I believe Ezra was a great man. That man had spiritual character. Whether it is in the company or whether it is in leadership, wherever it is and whatever form of ministry or responsibility we have, it is our spiritual, inward character that will give the character to everything else that we say and do in the finish, and will be our abiding influence after we have left the Earth. That will be the thing; it will be what we were inwardly.

Well, let's remember that together. It is severe. It is tremendous. It is deep, but it is part of this recovery. You have got the house recovered, you have got truth recovered, but you have got to have character recovered, too. It is no good having one without the other; you have got to have them both. So here is the second great movement of the return. A character is recovered and restored, not only in the people, but also in the leadership. May the Lord help us.

3.
A Review of the Book of Ezra

We have said at the beginning of this study that Ezra and Nehemiah are really most modern. Some scholars agree that I and II Chronicles, Ezra, and Nehemiah were originally one book. Even today in the Jewish Scripture, Ezra and Nehemiah are still one book. They were divided by Jerome and then later again divided so that we have them in their present arrangement as separate books. But nearly all good scholars agree that there is a joint authorship behind these volumes.

It is very difficult for us to put our finger on the person who is the author. Nowhere is he clearly named. Jewish tradition unhesitatingly ascribes the authorship of both Chronicles, Ezra, and Nehemiah to Ezra himself. There may be a lot to be said for Ezra's authorship. The only difficulties are two that are found in two places in the record and depend very largely on the high priest mentioned, particularly Jaddua. Another question is whether they are actually the sons and the grandsons of Nehemiah or whether they are his brothers. If we could only know the answers to those questions we would be much, much nearer to a clear understanding of who actually was the author of Chronicles, Ezra and Nehemiah.

However, of one thing we can be clear, which is that behind these books there is a common hand. There are, of course, the personal memoirs of Nehemiah and there are the personal memoirs of Ezra. Of course there are official documents and letters and so on that have been brought in, but there is just one common hand. You will remember all that we said in the first study upon these two books on the technical side.

The Great Value of Ezra and Nehemiah

Leaving the technical side for a moment, what is the real value of Ezra and Nehemiah? They of course can only be considered with Chronicles. For real understanding, spiritually intelligent understanding of them, they have got to be considered with Chronicles. They complete the overall picture, the birds eye view, or the overall survey of God's dealings with His people from Adam, to the coming of the Messiah. You will remember that many cases in Chronicles, Ezra and Nehemiah duplicate other material in the Word of God because they are written from a different standpoint to so much else in the Word of God. They are written to give us the key to God's eternal purpose, to give us, as it were, an interpretation of history from God's point of view. That is why Chronicles goes right back to Adam, and Nehemiah takes us right on to the coming of the Lord Jesus. So the whole of Old Testament history is comprehended by these books.

Then again, the greatest value of Ezra and Nehemiah is this: that as all Scripture in the Old Testament is given for our admonition upon whom the end of the ages have come, these things happened unto them in a figure. These things were given as an example for our admonition, our instruction, correction, alignment, however you would like to put it. All of the whole Old Testament can be summed up in it. We make a lot of the beginning of the Bible but very, very little of the end of the Bible. And we ought to see that the real value of Ezra/Nehemiah lies in this: that it contains principles that operate at the end of an age.

Ezra/Nehemiah is all to do with recovery. I think you all will remember, I reiterated it again and again, that the key to Chronicles, Ezra and Nehemiah is the house of God, the temple. That is the key. If you read a Roman Catholic commentary or Protestant commentary, you will find no other key given. Everyone, for once, is agreed that the key to Chronicles, Ezra and Nehemiah is the temple, the sanctuary, the dwelling place of God. Everyone is agreed. It is so obvious that I do not see how anyone could disagree. But Ezra and Nehemiah are one further step forward to Chronicles, in that the additional note is sounded of the recovery of the temple. Chronicles deals with the conception of the House of God, the actual building of the House of God, and the conflict over the House of God. But Ezra and Nehemiah deal with the recovery of the House of God. It therefore contains principles that are absolutely operative at the end of any dispensation when something original has been lost which the Holy Spirit is out to recover. Therein lies the real value of Ezra/Nehemiah. It embodies principles of recovery. Therefore we ought to take the more especial note of this two-fold book in the light of our own day and generation, and in the light of the coming of our Lord Jesus.

Here there are principles, not only operative in recovery of the temple or the House of God, but here there are principles that are operative in bringing in the Christ. Of course, people will disagree sometimes about this, but the Lord Jesus will not return to this earth 'willy-nilly,' any more than He came to this earth for the first time 'willy-nilly.' He did not come in a very abstract way. Certain conditions had to be fulfilled. Certain prophecies had to be fulfilled. A certain people in the earth had to be within certain boundaries. There had to be certain conditions, all of which had to be operative before the Lord Jesus could return. In the same way we understand that the Lord Jesus will not return for the second time just in any kind of way. He will return when certain conditions are fulfilled and when there are a certain people within certain spiritual boundaries in the right conditions. That is the real value of Ezra and Nehemiah. That is why I believe it has such a vitally important message for us in our study of it. We have got to understand that this spiritual book has within it the key to the end of a dispensation.

Well, that is all just the introduction really. It is a very, very simple little review of our rather bigger introduction to Ezra/Nehemiah, but there it is. It is something that needs to be stressed and reemphasised. Don't let us just come to this two-fold book in a kind of mentally interested way in the sense that it is just history. The Bible is not a history book. History is only found in the Scripture when it has something to teach us. Some people spend all their time trying to prove that God is true and God is right and what He has written is right and so on. In actual fact the

Lord Himself is the one who has presented this book of problems by the things He could have said and has not said, by the things He could have put in, and has not put in, and by the things perhaps that would have been better if He had left out, which He has not left out, but added. The Lord has helped the Modernists and the Higher Critics very greatly in their work in that sense because He is not bothered about whether men believe Him or do not believe Him. It does not make any difference to the truth of God, or anything about His purpose as to whether men believe or do not believe. God is sovereign in that respect. He has given us something in which every part is as important to the end in view, and therefore each part within the Word of God has something to teach us. History is not there as history, but because it embodies a principle or embodies something of very real importance for us in type or figure.

The Background

That is something about the beginning of this book and you will all remember something of the background of it. The people of God are in captivity. They have been in captivity 70 years. They were taken away by Nebuchadnezzar king of Babylon when Jerusalem was razed to the ground after a siege lasting three years, and then they were dispersed into different parts of the Babylonian empire. Strangely enough, after much cruelty, unhappiness, loss, and impoverishment, they were left completely in peace and began to settle down into little colonies of Jewry where they had their own rights, their own customs, their own language, their own everything. Strangely enough, as they settled down, they not only became respectable citizens but they began to dominate the commerce of the empire. As has always been the case, slowly but surely into their hands came the commerce of the whole empire.

Then we find that they not only became respectable, but they also became very prosperous. Then an even stranger thing happened to these Jewish exiles; they shunned the thing that had caused their exile. They refused to intermarry for the most part. They refused to get mixed up with the Gentiles in a whole number of ways. They became exclusive, tightly knit together colonies of Jewry and that is where the synagogues began. It was all very respectable and prosperous and peaceful. Seventy years later, due to the undying ministry of certain faithful men of God— Ezekiel, Daniel, Jeremiah, and so on—a little remnant was kept alive spiritually in a way that was peculiar, and distinguished them from the rest of their brothers and sisters. Then, after seventy years, you remember a largish group returned. They were for the most part penniless and impoverished. Mostly they went on foot, but they returned back to the homeland. Their one aim, and indeed the decree of King Cyrus was that they should rebuild the house of God which is in Jerusalem. That was the whole point of their return: that they might rebuild the dwelling place of God.

You remember in the background that the Babylonian Empire had given way for the Persian Empire and this is one of the most dramatic and remarkable changes in the history of the ancient world. For the Babylonians were entirely different from the Persians in every way, not only in racial origin, but in much else, particularly in worship. Whereas the Babylonians believed in a multitude of gods and divine beings and so on, the

Persians believed in the unity of the godhead who could never be represented by any image or anything at all. The only symbol that god had was fire. That was the only visible symbol of his presence. They were called Zoroastrians. Because of their religion, because of their attitude to life they of course had a natural affinity to the Jew. Therefore, the whole attitude to the Jewish exile was changed in the sovereignty of God. Well, that is all the background.

The Three Returns

The return was in three parts. The first return under Zerubbabel is recorded in the first six chapters of Ezra. The second return under Ezra was about 60–70 years later and numbered probably about three thousand people. (The first was something like 42,000–43,000 people). The third return was under Nehemiah and was a very small company indeed and that was twelve years later than the return under Ezra. The interesting thing that emerges is that as the exile took place in three clearly defined stages, so the return to the land was in three clearly defined stages. It is very interesting.

What did we learn under the first return? We see that in this whole question of the recovery of the dwelling place of God, the house of God, the Lord wants to teach us three very clear things. He has defined these principles in this three-fold return. Now you will understand that we will pass over the main points that we have already considered very swiftly. I am leaving quite a lot out and will be taking up just one or two points and dwelling on them. I know it is a bit much sometimes having to go over what you have already heard. However, I understand that reiteration is the basis of good teaching, so it may be that this will help everyone.

The Recovery of Truth in Practice

Under the first return led by Zerubbabel in Ezra 1–6, we found that the first thing the Holy Spirit brings into view is the recovery of truth in practice. I think this is most important—the recovery of truth in practice. May I put it another way? Reality. Wherever you find the word truth in Scripture it does not merely mean truth as something written or as a teaching. The word means something more than a teaching. It means reality. It means what is true, what is truth about anything. It is not necessarily something in writing. It is not necessarily a doctrine. Truth is the reality about anything. That is truth.

The Holy Spirit teaches us under the first return led by Zerubbabel the recovery of truth in practice. That is, there is a sphere of truth. As Paul writes to Timothy, he spoke of the church as the pillar and ground (or bulwark) of truth, of reality. He spoke of a sphere of reality outside of which you can have good things and right things, but they would not be, as it were, judged. You might get lop-sided, unbalanced. Do you understand? You could have a lot that was right and true and real, but there is a sphere in which all that is judged and exposed. The first thing the Holy Spirit teaches us in this whole question of recovery is that He is after, first of all, the recovery of truth in practice. Now, this question of truth in practice *is* the house of God. The whole first six chapters of Ezra deal with the house of God, or the temple, or the sanctuary, or if you like another title, the dwelling place of God. We call it *the Church*, the recovery of the Church.

The Ground

Now as I said a little while ago, we are not going to literally dwell on every point that we took in our previous study. I want to just draw out the four things that we see as absolutely vital that are contained in the first six chapters of Ezra. In the recovery of the church, the first thing the Holy Spirit focuses down upon is the question of ground. Of course we could go through a whole number of verses right through these six chapters, but if we take just three verses, Ezra 1:2—4, we read this, "... he hath charged me to build him a house in Jerusalem. ... let him go up to Jerusalem, which is in Judah, and build the house of the Lord, the God of Israel ... which is in Jerusalem. And whosoever is left, in any place where he sojourneth, let the men of his place help him with silver, and with gold, and with goods, and with beasts, besides the freewill-offering for the house of God which is in Jerusalem."

If you read through those chapters you will become almost tired of this little phrase "the house of God which is in Jerusalem." This is all the more amazing because this book, this record was written after the children of Israel were back in the land and when they were dwelling once again in Jerusalem. So it is all the more remarkable that the Holy Spirit has reiterated and reemphasised this question of the house of God which is in Jerusalem, all the time "... which is in Jerusalem." The whole tragedy of the division of the people of God into Judah and Israel was over the question of the house of God—where the house of God should be, where God should dwell.

Therefore, the first thing we see about the recovery of truth in practice is this: it is a question of ground. Christianity asks, "What are you?" Brother Nee says we ought to ask, "Where are you?" The two things are as necessary. It is most remarkable that the first question the Holy Spirit asks is, "Where are you?" and not, "What are you?" So we find there is a question of ground. What does that mean in practical terms in the twentieth century? It means simply this: you cannot build the church where you want. You cannot build it just anywhere. There is clearly defined ground upon which alone the house of God can be built. What is this ground? Well, I will first speak of it spiritually. This ground is Christ, simply Christ. It is not a teaching. It is not national. It is not racial. It is not social. It is not a question of it being built on certain forms of church government or certain rights or ceremonies, or practices. The church can only be found on the ground of Christ.

But we must go one step further. Where is Christ found? According to the New Testament we find Christ in our locality— you will not find a single instance of any church anywhere except on the ground of its locality. There is the church of God at Ephesus, the church of God at Corinth, the church of God at Rome, the churches in Judea and so on. It is always on the ground of their locality. There were never two churches in one locality. If you search the whole of the New Testament, you will not find two churches in one locality. They were always referred to as "*the* church at ..." The church at Jerusalem met in a whole number of different homes because it was so large. It had to, but it was still only *the* church at Jerusalem. In other words, there could only be one church to one locality. This church was built on what Christ is, and found by saints, resident within that locality. That is what we mean by church ground, and the first thing the Holy Spirit speaks of here in symbol and type is that the house of God could only be built in a certain place.

You will remember that this can be traced through Deuteronomy. Here, first of all, the Lord began to say: Make sure, that when you come into the land you do not build the house of God where you wish, where you desire, nor do you offer your burnt offerings or your sacrifices or your vows where you wish, but you will come to the place where I will choose to cause my name to dwell there and there I will accept your offerings and your vows, and so on (see Dt. 12). The Old Testament is almost comprehended by this simple fact of where God chose His name to dwell. You could build wonderful edifices anywhere else in the world, but they were not the house of God, and God would not dwell there. You could build them in Babylon and you could build them in Egypt. You could build them in other beautiful places. You could build them in a place called Bethel, which means "the house of God," which Israel did. However, it is still not the house of God and God will not dwell there. He may meet you there, as He did at Bethel. He may speak to His prophets there. You may have experiences there of God, but God will not dwell there. He will only dwell in one place and that place is Jerusalem. Now we are children of the Jerusalem which is above, but still today it is exactly the same. It is this that Christianity has lost sight of. It has left the one ground of unity which it is possible to have worldwide (for those of us who love and know the Lord), and have exchanged it for that kind of basis, which issues and results in a million fragments, divisions, sects, and so on. It is a tragedy.

So, we find that this question of ground is stressed at the very beginning in this whole question of truth being recovered in practice. You see what the Lord is first saying here is very simple. The first thing God will do when He starts to move is to see that we are gathered on the right ground. It is no good trying to build the house of God anywhere else. I know (and I bet you do as well) of many groups and companies here in this country and elsewhere that have got what they call "New Testament patterns." Everything is New Testament pattern. They have tried to return as clearly as possible to the New Testament and have set up a New Testament pattern. When they have done it all and they ask the Lord to bless it, they cannot understand why the Lord will not commit Himself. Today there are many people leaving, many young people leaving New Testament patterns. They are disillusioned, quite disillusioned because somehow or other the Lord will not commit Himself with the New Testament pattern. Why will He not commit Himself? It is because it is not a question of New Testament pattern. It is a question of Christ found on the ground of our locality. The pattern is in the life of Christ. You cannot just find it and build on it. That is very important. We have to understand that.

Another thing connected with this is that nowhere in the Scripture, particularly here in Ezra and Nehemiah, will you ever find quite the same thing holding good at the end of a dispensation as it did at the beginning. You will find that there is a principle with God. It is what we could call a remnant principle. (I cannot think of any other word to describe it.) It is simply this: that at the end of every dispensation there is only a remnant. Isn't that interesting? God starts off with a race, and it ends with Noah and seven other people. Right the way through, if you trace at the end of every single Old Testament age or dispensation, you have only a handful left out of a great number. It is so with the New Testament age. We began with all; we shall end with a remnant. Now that does not mean that all those who are the Lord's are cut off from the Lord. It does not mean that at all. If you read the Scriptures very carefully, you will find that they were still the Lord's though they still remained in exile. But there was always only a remnant that returned. It seems to be almost a principle with the Lord. All the prophets speak about the remnant that, in the end, returns. So it is, even if you look at the book of Revelation, which corresponds to the prophecies of the Old Testament. You will find the result of the prophecy is that that every one ends with an overcomer. That is all. It narrows down. It does not mean that the others lose their salvation; they do not. But those that are found at the end, on the original basis, are few.

Here in Ezra chapter two, you will find the genealogy of those that return. It was a very small remnant of a great nation. Only a small number have come back. So we can only expect to find a small number on this ground at the end. We cannot expect all the Lord's people to return to that ground. The cost is too great. There is far too much prosperity and satisfaction with things as they are for there to be a great number that return to such ground. But there will be those that do return.

The Altar

Then you will notice in Ezra 3:3, that we find the altar is mentioned. This is the second thing about the first return. The first was ground; the second is the altar. The cross is primary to anything of the church in expression. The first thing we must do if we would know the church of God recovered, if we would know the house of God recovered, is to get a number of people onto the right ground. The second thing is for the altar to be put into its place, that is, for the cross to be operative in the life of that group. When you get the cross operative in the lives of that group, something starts to happen. Calvary always precedes Pentecost. Not only historically, but always in experience. You can never become part of the church, you can never contribute in the church, you can never become, as it were, knitted into the body of the Lord Jesus without a deep, experiential knowledge of the cross.

The altar is the first thing, practically, after the ground. First, God defines the ground under Zerubbabel: "Jerusalem. You cannot build My house anywhere else. You go back to Jerusalem and you can build the house there." However, before ever the foundation is laid, before ever they mark out the site, before ever they start to quarry the stones or get the timber, the first thing to be put into place is the altar. The brazen altar is put into its place. Furthermore, upon the brazen altar are offered burnt offerings and sacrifices. Before ever a stone is put upon a stone, before ever the materials are got there and prepared, the cross is operative. The altar is in working order and being used. Isn't that a most significant thing? It simply means this: getting a group of people onto the ground of Christ in their localities, is in some ways an easy thing, but to get the altar into that people, and those people onto that altar is a very difficult thing. Sometimes you will find that we have succeeded in the first and failed in the second, yet everything is essential. For there is absolutely no doubt whatsoever, that until we come to terms with the cross of our Lord Jesus there can be no church in expression whatsoever.

If you feel that you are not really functioning, or not really part of what God is doing, then you must look not to others, but to the cross in your life. The easiest thing of all and the cheapest thing to do is to blame others. That is what people always do. They say, "Oh, no one cares about me. No one bothers about me. No one goes out for me. No one sort of looks after me," and all the rest of it. Well, maybe those things are very true. But if everyone showed you all the love and care and affection they possibly could, that would not make you one whit more of the church. Not one whit! All it would do is to thoroughly deceive you. Because you are surrounded by affection and all those kinds of things, you would think you are part of it when you are not. That is why it is the most difficult thing in the world to make a person realise they are loved and wanted when they obviously are, but they have got it right into their being that they are not.

I tell you why: because the Holy Spirit has put it in there. The Holy Spirit will put a divine veto upon any sense of your being wanted or loved until you come to terms with the cross. This is the most thoroughly heartbreaking business of all, this question of coming to terms with the cross. To come right down to it, we have to say, "Well, if no one wants me, if no one loves me, if no one is prepared to draw me in, if no one is prepared to speak to me, if no one is prepared to help me, I am on this ground and I am going to go out to everyone else." However, the first thing you have to do is come to terms with the cross. There is no use trying to get around it. As I said, the cheapest thing to do is to blame your dear brothers and sisters and the more you blame your dear brothers and sisters the harder you make it for yourself. Without a doubt you just make it more, and more, and more difficult.

No, it is a question of the altar. But first thing, before ever the stones are there, the wood is there, the materials are there, the vessels are there or anything else is there, it is the altar that is put into its place and something is offered up. You and I must understand that before ever there can be any church in expression, we have got to get a people onto this right ground and then get them onto the altar. When we do that we have got the first, primary thing that is absolutely necessary for anything to happen.

May I say this further thing upon this matter because this is so practical? I suppose there is not a soul in this room that has not got this as their problem: this question of being loved and wanted. I might just say this. It is just there that the Holy Spirit puts His finger upon our self-centredness in its deepest and in many ways most intangible form.

You see, we talk again and again when we preach the gospel about self-centredness being sin. That is sin. That gives rise to everything. These people come to the Lord. They come to know the Lord. They come into a knowledge of their forgiveness. They are cleansed. But still this ghastly, evil, perverted thing lingers on under the surface until it is brought to the cross. It is this which rips at you. Rips any going on with the Lord and rips all that in half. Oh, it is only self. Make no bones about it whatsoever. When next you feel like that, you can tell yourself,

"All this is is self-centredness with a capital 'S.'" The Lord will give you a bigger, and bigger, and bigger dose of it until, at last, you come to the question that the easiest thing to do, quite frankly, is to put it all on the altar. Either you will go away, or you will come to the altar. That is what happens, one of those two alternatives.

So, we find the altar there. The altar is the thing that governs everything. When you have the altar in its place, then everything else begins to develop. You will find this again, and again everywhere through Scripture in types, in shadow, and later on in the New Testament, in practice, but it is there.

The Foundation

The third thing that we find, and I am going to pass over quite simply, is Ezra 3:10. After we have got the ground, after we have got the altar, the next thing we find is the foundation. That is an interesting thing. The foundation is laid after the altar. Isn't that interesting? The foundation comes after the altar. What is this foundation? We are told in the New Testament what the foundation is. There is a foundation, which is laid, which is Christ. God has laid this foundation. It is the Lord Jesus Christ Himself. We are told elsewhere that the Lord Jesus is the chief cornerstone, and the prophets and apostles are the other stones. They are together the foundation. Do you understand? It is really all Christ. It is the foundation. What is the foundation? I will tell you what the foundation is. The foundation is a primary and essential experience of Christ, corporately as our life and oneness. Now, this is very interesting. Before ever there can be any recovery of the house of God or the Church in fulness, there must be a primary experience of Christ corporately, as our life and oneness.

What does this mean? It means that when you have got a people on the right ground, on Christ in their locality, they have taken that ground clearly, and they refuse to take any other ground, or to leave it. They are staying there, whatever they find out about one another or about anything else. They are staying there on that ground. That is the only ground they can see. They have got to stay there or lose everything. When they see the altar and come to the altar, the very next thing is this: they start to find themselves being introduced, in an elementary way, into a knowledge of Christ as their corporate life and oneness.

This will explain a tremendous amount for many of us. Why do we have those terribly dark times that sometimes last for months and sometimes for years, of suspicion and reservation about the rest, about our other brothers and sisters? Why is it that the Lord allows seemingly so much evidence for things? Why is it that we are always, as it were, the centre and the recipient of so much trouble? What is it the Lord is trying to do? All He is trying to do is to bring us to the place where we can distinguish what is Christ and what is not Christ in myself, and in one another. In other words, we come to this elementary experience of Christ as our corporate life and unity in this way: we say as Paul says, "I determine not to know anything among you, save Jesus Christ and Him crucified." That is, Paul says, "The only thing I touch in my brothers and sisters is a crucified Christ, what has been produced by a knowledge of Christ crucified. The rest, well I know how rotten it is, so I won't bother about it."

That is a great place to come to, but no one comes there theoretically. You won't get there in a Bible college either. You may be taught it, but it won't come to you in experience. You will only come to that when you are knocked all over the place by your brothers and sisters. You are so knocked all over the place that you come to the point where you think, "I am going to leave. I am just fed up with them all." But then you find that there is this strange fear in your heart, of committing a kind of spiritual sin now. Then you think, "Oh dear. I have got to stay here. I cannot leave them. Oh, oh, what a terrible thing! I have to stay with them." For a while it is grim and dark and terrible until we discover that what we are seeing now, is exactly ourselves in them. It is Jacob and Laban. When they come and they pour out their troubles about so-and-so did this and so-and-so did that and the other. Well, sometimes it turns out that all they retold and all they have now passed on to me is a perfect picture of themselves.

So that is how we come to it—an essential experience of Christ as our life and unity. There comes a place where either we go— or we stay. If we stay, we take Christ as our life and unity and something happens. We are forged[1]. I cannot explain it any other way. It comes by the cross. Men and women who lay down their lives and are then suddenly forged. They can hear the same old stories about one another and they know they are true (some of them) and they say, "Well, I know this; I know that. However, I have been forged into what is of Christ in these people and they have been forged into what is of Christ in me, however small."

So, you see, the church, I might say, is the ground and the pillar of the reality. Do you understand that? Reality. It is not that

1 Forged as in "being forged in the fire"

mindless Christian idealism which pictures a beautiful lovely thing up there where all is sweet fellowship and service and harmony and order and everyone loves everyone else. It is all so very, very beautiful. That is what we paint so often and everyone thinks, "Oh dear, they are all hypocrites. They are hypocrites! I say, they are hypocrites."

Brother Lee described to me, the work in Formosa as seamy,[2] and I have never, anywhere heard anyone describe the work of God on earth as seamy. I was quite taken aback. I have since thought it over a lot. That is the only person I have ever heard describe a work in which he was engaged in real terms. When the cross works and when the Holy Spirit begins to work, things become very seamy. Things come out, things come up, and things come to the surface. Everything becomes real. Oh, when we first come and look at them, they are such saints, such perfect saints. Look how they pray. Look how they talk to each other. Then we get to know them, we find that so-and-so is very irritable. We find so-and-so is jealous. Ah, but so-and-so wants to get through, and they are getting through; but still, they are irritable—while they are getting through and they are jealous—while they are getting through. There are many other things, while they are they getting through. So often, as the Holy Spirit deals with people, all these things that are ugly and vile come up to the surface. All we can see is the scum on the surface. Sometimes we lose sight of what God is doing underneath in that person because we can only see what is clouding the vision.

---

2 Definition of *seamy*
  2a: UNPLEASANT b: DEGRADED, SORDID
  https://www.merriam-webster.com/dictionary/seamy - other-words

This is an essential experience of Christ as the foundation. There will never be the Church built until the Lord gets a people forged with such a foundation. Never. Never! You and I should all pack up now. You will never have the Church with all its wonderful ministries, functions, and so on, until Christ has got a foundation like that. The altar and the foundation. Once you have that you have got everything. Oh, to get such a foundation. But there you are, this is recovery of truth in practice of the house of God, the dwelling place of Christ.

You see, may I put it like this? The whole question of the Church down here is like a kindergarten, as it were. It is the sphere of the Church up there, formed. What is going up there? There is no scum, no seaminess, nothing impure, no blemish, no fault. Down here, we are conscious of all the other side of it, but it is down here that what goes up there is produced, not in some lovely, little secluded spot of peace, with singing and birds twittering. It is produced here, with our "very ugly" brothers and sisters. Here is where the real work is done, and where the gold is produced—down here. So you understand there is a lot to work on here, isn't there?

The House of God Produced

Lastly, we find in this first return the question of the house of God, *actually*. Oh yes, it is here that the house of God is produced when we have got such a foundation. It all goes up, though there is a lot of opposition ... and you do have a lot of opposition in there. Remember we studied back and forth about it—all the opposition to getting the house of God really going up and being complete, but it never stopped it. When the Lord has got a foundation, you cannot stop the work. You can stop it for a little while, but you cannot stop it completely. The essential thing is ground, an altar, and a foundation.

The trouble with modern day Christianity is it is trying to bypass the first three and get to the end. It may stay perfect for a little while, but just wait until a few storms come. You cannot have Pentecost without Calvary. That is the tragedy of so much that is prevalent amongst us who are the Lord's people. Well, there we are. That is the first return.

The Recovery of Inward Character

What about the second return? The second return covers the last four chapters of Ezra. What does the second return deal with? You remember it was under Ezra and there were only about 3,000 people. Now, here is the interesting thing: you remember, everything in these four chapters, seven through ten of Ezra, is to do with inward character. Building is not mentioned at all. We do not get an instance of actual building. Only in his prayer is the recovery of the house of God and the wall in Jerusalem mentioned. That is all. In actual fact we get nothing mentioned at all about a building. It is all a question of inward character.

Now, let us mark this very carefully. This underlines the absolute necessity of spiritual inward character. It is a great mistake if we swing to the other extreme and say, "It is all just a question of getting people onto the ground. It is not a question of spirituality. Spirituality is a thing that we have been taught, and taught, and taught, and taught. It is a question of getting people onto the right ground." No, no. That is true, but it is an absolute necessity to have inward spiritual character. The second return is all to do with the recovery of an inward character in the people who return. Things were in a very poor way. You have got the people back in the land. Do you see what I mean? You have got them back in Jerusalem. The house of God is rebuilt. The services are in progress, but you have not got an inward character. The people have got a marriage problem, and so we could go on. The whole thing is a mess.

This second return is all to do with the question of the recovery of inward spiritual character. However, and I want you to underline this in your heart, not your notebook, but in your heart: *the Holy Spirit here is teaching us the correct order in recovery.* That is the most important thing of all! We must note the order that the Holy Spirit has placed these things in. First, is recovery of truth in practice, then the recovery of inward character. First, get the people onto right ground, get the altar, get the house of God. Then, we will have inward spiritual character.

Now, I want you to note first of all the Holy Spirit's order. I am not being critical, but I believe only truthful. You must also note the present day inversion of that order. You see Christianity today speaks of spirituality, of inward spiritual character as being the beginning and the end of everything and in that, many of us would agree, I at least, unto its necessity. But they speak of it as the beginning and the end of everything. Christianity today says, "It does not matter where you go in the world, or where you worship, or to what you belong, so long as you are a little broad. So long as you do not get too narrow, it does not matter to what you belong. The real point is, you must have something broad.

The real point is spirituality. Let's forget what you belong to. Let's forget where you worship. It does not matter."

Do you see? Now, I am speaking of the best streams of evangelical Christianity: "It does not matter. Let us not divide over where you belong or what you do, or that kind of thing. The whole point is inward character. Inward character." (I am not speaking of narrow, exclusive, closed circles.) The best exponent and the most blessed interpreter of this is Keswick. It is wonderful. The whole point of Keswick is: "Let people come from all their different connections and places, but the point we want is to get an inward spiritual character." Now, that is all very, very wonderful.

Then, let us also make this point: uprightness, holiness, righteousness, godliness, and spirituality are of great gain. It does not matter in what you are. I say this, and it might horrify some of you. If you are a born again believer, it does not matter if you are a Roman Catholic (and there are many Roman Catholics who are born again). If you have got something about you which is godly, and something about you which is upright, and something that is true spiritual character it is profitable eternally. It does not matter where or with what you are connected or where you belong. What is of Christ in every one is profitable forever.

But let us also say this: our righteousness is not necessary to God. We make a big mistake if we think it is necessary to God that we should be righteous. By that I mean that our uprightness somehow qualifies God; it does not do anything of the kind! If God committed us all to hell it would not make a single difference to His own holiness and righteousness. He does not *need* our godliness; He does not need our righteousness, as if He is in *need* of our godliness. He is, Himself, sufficient. Therefore, you mark this: to be godly, to be spiritual, to be Christ-like and, as it were, just to be an individual floating around in the earth is of great gain to us, but of no gain to God. It is valuable for us, eternally, but not valuable to Him. But, if God can get saints gathered on the right ground, with an inward spiritual character, it is as much gain to Him as it is to us, for they will become His dwelling place, eternally. They can be knitted in to what He is doing. They become members of one body, members of each other, fused together. That is the whole point.

That is why the Holy Spirit gives us this order. First, He speaks of the recovery of truth in practice. You see? The house of God. Then He speaks of inward character. When we have it that way 'round, we are safe. Just think of it. When God gets inward character on that ground it is corrected and preserved, and you are saved from those deceptions that can quickly grow. So, you see it is all a very, very remarkable thing that the whole of these four chapters is to do with this question of inward character. The first thing the Holy Spirit says is, I have got a people on the right ground. Now, the next thing to do is to see that there is an inward character there.

What is the real heart of this inward character? The thing the Holy Spirit focuses His attention right down on is mixed marriage. What is mixed marriage? Why all this talk about mixed marriage? Why this seeming harshness and severity on the part of Ezra over this question of mixed marriage? It is because this question of mixed marriage goes to the heart of inward character. It goes to our failures. It goes to the deepest part of our being, the part that so often is the most unyielding. When that is dealt with, spiritual character is produced and only then. That is the heart of true spiritual character.

Many of us are prepared to serve the Lord, so long as *those* things are not really dealt with. We are prepared to go quite a way with the Lord, so long as those things are not brought to the cross. But this question of inward character is the exact thing that has to be touched by the Holy Spirit. When *that* is touched by the Holy Spirit, then you have the character being developed. That means severity and, of course, discipline—the discipline and the severity of the handling of God.

It is remarkable when you read Hebrews 12, those amazing words about the Lord receiving sons. These sons will be chastened. He chastises, He disciplines (disciplines is the word), He trains, in a rather severe, strong way—as children. It goes on to say as we have often quoted, "He scourges every son whom He loveth." Whom He loveth, He chastens and scourges every son whom He receiveth. Well, that speaks of severe handling, doesn't it? Scourging, you know, is not just chastening. It is one thing to be smacked across the knuckles by your father for plucking some flower which you should have never plucked in the garden. It is another thing altogether to be thoroughly whipped—to be scourged. It says that the Father *chastises*, that is, you see, to get many raps over the knuckles. We are disciplined on many occasions because He loves us. But also there are times when we get a thorough hiding because He is receiving us. He is accepting us as sons. In other words, He has got a place to which He is receiving us—a responsible position in the household to which He is bringing us. So we get a thoroughly good hiding down here. Do you understand?

That is all to do with inward spiritual character. Proverbs says, "Spare the rod and spoil the child." That is true, isn't it? It is spiritually true, anyway. Now, the Lord does not spare the rod and spoil His children. We have the rod, and a certain kind of child is put to it. So, let us remember this. We will leave it there.

We have reviewed the whole book of Ezra. There is a lot in it to think about. There is the question of this recovery of truth and also the question of the recovery of an inward character. Only the Lord can interpret those things to you and to me, to give us a real understanding of what they mean practically. The Lord does not just want an inward spiritual character *anywhere* connected with *anything*. He wants to get us onto the ground of Christ. Then, once He has got us onto this ground, He wants to produce in us an inward character.

4.
The Third Return Under Nehemiah

We come to the third and final section of Ezra and Nehemiah. This section falls naturally into the heading in Scripture, "The Third Return Under Nehemiah." This whole part of Ezra/Nehemiah, this book that we call the book of Nehemiah in actual fact is the second part of this work, and is completely taken up with the third return. It is very interesting because in this particular party under Nehemiah, there were not very many that did return. It was the smallest of the groups that would return. We do not actually know the number but it would have been quite a small selective group and this whole book of Nehemiah covers the third stage of the return to the land.

Before we actually look at this third stage of the return, if we are going to understand anything at all, we need to ask ourselves what the walls are. What do the walls really mean? It is perfectly clear that the third stage of the return is wholly to do with the walls of Jerusalem. This book of Nehemiah is completely taken up with the walls. The first seven chapters are exclusively dealing with the walls. First of all, you get the burden about the walls, then Nehemiah going to review the walls, and then after the review of the walls, you get the commencement of the actual building of the walls. Then there is the conflict over the walls. Then, at last, you get the completion of the walls. That is found within the first seven chapters of Nehemiah.

In Nehemiah thirteen there is the dedication of the walls, so that this part of Ezra/Nehemiah, is taken up completely with the walls. Even the other chapters, Nehemiah eight through twelve, are really in some way connected with the walls. The walls are not actually mentioned in those chapters but they are bounded by the dedication. It is very interesting that the dedication of the walls comes so late in the record so that we have other matters coming before. Then, of course, the last chapter, chapter thirteen, is to do with the final clearing up of one or two matters in the city. So we can see straightaway that this part of this work of the chronicler is all to do with the walls.

In the first return, we found that we were dealing with the house of God. We were dealing with the house of God in every aspect—its ground, its foundation, its structure, the way that it is produced, the cross, and so on. In the first stage of the return every single aspect is to do with the house of God—from the actual ground that must be returned to, to the foundation that has got to be laid, to the altar that must receive even the foundation, to the structure that at last is completed after much conflict. Everything in that first return under Zerubbabel and Jeshua, is to do with the house of God.

In the second return, everything is to do with inward moral character. Here, God would have us put first the very question of the recovery of truth in practice. When we have got that clear and we return to certain ground and understand something of God's purpose, then the Holy Spirit gets down to this business of inward spiritual character. Evangelical Christianity has inverted the order and put first inward spiritual character, and then these other things. However, it is clear from the Word of God that the first thing is the ground, then the foundation, and then the altar. The next thing that is recovered in this three-fold recovery, this restoration of the people of God to the land, is inward spiritual character.

The Lord's Work in the Third Return

Having established this, and having on the one side gone back to certain ground, and having seen something of God's purpose and His goal, and having seen also the very real necessity of spiritual character, going hand in hand with the other, now we come to this question of the wall. The third return is the more remarkable because it is all to do with the wall, when so much of the actual city has not been rebuilt. This simply means that the walls were completed before the actual buildings within the city were completed.

Now, do take note of that order. First, God gets the group going back, the largest group going back, but still a remnant, and they erect the altar on that ground and then they build the house of God on that ground. The next real thing is, of course, a question of spiritual character, the spiritual character of the people. Then, the third and final stage in recovery is the wall, a wall to the city. It is most interesting when we really note something of that order.

The Meaning of Walls

When we come to the third part of the return, we come to that which is much fuller than the other two. The other two as we have already said, were dealing with very, very important and vital matters. However, when we come to the walls we come to something which is an expansion of anything that has preceded it. The walls gather up everything that has been recovered. The Hebrew word for walls is simply enclosure, that which encloses and the walls enclose everything which has now been recovered and restored. It is the fullest stage of the recovery, as you would expect, being the last.

The wall encloses, first of all, a city. At the heart of that city there is the temple. These walls then enclose that. In actual fact, much of the city itself would be built after the wall. But the point is that the walls enclose a city and at the heart of that city there is the dwelling place of God. That may give us some idea when we come to ask ourselves the question, "What do the walls really symbolise?" If the Holy Spirit takes up so much time on this question of the walls, what do they really symbolise, recognising that these walls enclose, first of all, certain ground? I trust that is very clear, to everyone. These walls are built on the perimeter of a certain ground, which is called Jerusalem. Everything within those walls is Jerusalem and everything outside those walls is not Jerusalem.

Therefore, first of all those walls enclose a certain ground. They are put there as a permanent boundary of the ground where God has chosen to cause His name to dwell. Those walls are a permanent, solid, clear boundary. That is the first thing.

The walls enclose certain ground which God has chosen out of all the localities of the promised land. Out of everything He could have chosen, He chose the place called Jerusalem to cause His name to dwell there. That was to be the place of His dwelling.

Secondly, it encloses the temple. It not only encloses ground bigger than the temple, but it actually encloses the house of God upon that ground. Within those walls, not outside those walls, but within those walls is the very dwelling place of God on earth. Under the old covenant this was the actual spot in the whole of inhabited earth where God literally dwelt. He was found by His people there.

Thirdly, these walls enclosed a city, which was to become a centre of authority, of government, and of administration. We recognise all that as being enclosed by the walls of Jerusalem. We learn, therefore, that there are three things that we can say about the wall.

The Walls As Definition

What do the walls symbolise? We can say, first, obviously there is definition. The walls symbolise definition. They define something. They define something which is abundantly clear. They put a boundary between what is not God's ground and what is God's ground. They define where God can be found and where He cannot be found. They define a place of authority. There is no other place that God has chosen to be the centre of government and authority and administration in His land. This is the place from which God said He would rule the earth. Those walls then define something.

So, the first thing we say about walls (and of course this is true of any wall) the wall in the garden, apart from anything else is a definition. It defines ground which belongs to us. It is on the boundary. It defines something.

The Walls As Separation

Secondly, that wall is a wall of separation. This of course is linked very closely with definition. But it is a wall that does divide. It ensures a purity. That is the point. What is within those enclosed walls was kept, as it were, enclosed. It was guarded. It was separate. It could not just go on growing and growing and growing—spreading out. Those walls, and particularly in the days of which we are speaking, meant safety to everyone inside. They separated a certain city. They separated a certain place. It speaks therefore of separation. Walls in the Scripture always speak of separation. You remember in the Song of Solomon, he speaks of the Church being a walled garden. Always walls speak of this separation, not only something defined, but something separate.

By the way, there are very few other walls taken up in Scripture the way the walls of Jerusalem are to the very end of the Bible. In the very last chapters of the Bible there is a lot about the walls of the New Jerusalem. They speak of something which is separate unto God. Even if we believe that there will be a kingdom of God, and there will be nations in that kingdom, we see that the city of God is something which is peculiarly first fruits unto God. It is very interesting, as we shall see later on in Nehemiah eleven, that it was a tenth of the nation that dwelt within those walls, only a tenth, and those who freely offered themselves though there were not very many of them. However, a tenth was taken, one in ten. What does this mean? It just means first fruits. You see? Jerusalem, is first fruits unto God. It is something peculiarly separated unto God.

The Walls As Preservation

We not only see that but we see these walls speak of preservation. Definition, separation, preservation. Walls in the old days preserved a people. It preserved a character. Even today, some of you, now and again perhaps, go to a city and there is a wall (though there are not many left in this country) and we still see a little that has been preserved because of the wall. Whenever you find walls completely intact, there is usually a certain atmosphere preserved within those walls.

These walls stand for preservation, the conservation of something, and the preservation of something that God has given and yes, you could say it is protection. It is being guarded. But better still, conserved—here is a place in which everything is conserved. John Newton knew a good deal more than many of us today when he said[1]: "Saviour, if of Zion's city I, thro' grace, a member am," and then he went on to speak about so "many joys and lasting treasure none but Zion's children know." It is within these walls, you see, that something is conserved and preserved.

The Testimony of Jesus

So, when we come to this question of the wall if we take these three things—definition, separation, preservation—we can sum

1 John Newton's hymn, *Glorious Things of Thee Are Spoken*

it all up in one word: testimony. This word testimony sums this up. It is something defined. It is a testimony to something clearly defined. It is a testimony of something separate, of an all-together different order, something essentially different to any other city on the earth. It speaks of something which is eternal, something which enjoys the guardianship of God. It enjoys the actual personal care of the Lord.

So, what do these walls really symbolise? They symbolise that which we have come to know in the New Testament as the testimony of Jesus. These walls are but the symbol of that, and all that that means. (If you want to know what the testimony of Jesus is you must read the book of Revelation and there you will find something of the testimony of Jesus.)

What is the testimony of Jesus? Is the testimony of Jesus just ministry? Is the testimony of Jesus just work? Is the testimony of Jesus just (and I must be careful) a life? The testimony of Jesus, we are told in Scripture is symbolised by a golden lampstand. And this golden lampstand is the Church. The testimony of Jesus is intimately bound up with the churches. This is why the book of Revelation begins with the seven churches—seven golden lampstands in the mist of which the Lord Himself walked.

At the end of the book of Revelation, the seven churches have given way to the one city. No more are the churches mentioned, only now will there remain a city. This city is called the lampstand of the nations. It contains the glory of God. It is the light of the universe. There is no need of the sun, no need of the moon, no need of anything else that we call light; it is itself the light, the eternal light of the universe. What was at the beginning of the book linked with believers on earth in different localities now has been transformed into something which is eternal, which has eternal vocation, and which is going to last throughout eternity. That is the testimony of Jesus.

The book of Revelation corresponds in many ways to Ezra/Nehemiah in the sense that it seeks to portray the terrible conflict raging over the testimony of Jesus from the day of Pentecost down through to the coming of our Lord Jesus Christ. It depicts the mortal conflict of Satan to destroy those that hold the testimony of Jesus and to overthrow and compromise it. How can he compromise it? By getting right at the essential nature of that testimony. That testimony is linked with the Church of God expressed on earth. You can have all the Christian work in the world that you want. You can have all the Christian experience in the world that you can muster. But if you haven't got the church of God expressed in the earth, you cannot have the testimony of Jesus. The lampstand is not associated with ones and twos here and there, on just any kind of ground, in any kind of thing. It is associated with those who have taken a certain ground and are found on a certain foundation by the deep working of the cross. They have been loosed from their sins in His blood. They have overcome the devil by His blood and by the word of their testimony, loving not their lives unto the death. These are people, you see, who have held, from the beginning to the end to certain truth. I hesitate to use that word, but you understand what I mean. When I say a certain truth, I really mean the testimony of Jesus. The book of Revelation is the record of those who in every age have held the testimony of Jesus and what it has meant. They have met the full blast of the enemy.

So, these walls symbolise what? The testimony of Jesus. Therefore they are of the most vital, vital, importance to us. For Nehemiah does not speak just of the testimony of Jesus. He speaks, he symbolises, he, as it were, portrays or foreshadows the recovery of the testimony of Jesus. Most real Bible scholars will agree that the testimony of Jesus is not here. It does not matter what denomination or where they are found, they all agree the testimony of Jesus has been lost. So we are faced in the end days of the New Testament age with this whole question of the recovery of the testimony of Jesus.

The Time of Nehemiah and the Prophets

Now, let's get back to Nehemiah. These walls gather up all that has preceded. They are, as it were, the last stage in a recovery. The first stage was the house of God. The second stage was inward character. The third stage was the testimony of Jesus. It is not just the house of God as the dwelling place of God, but it is the city of God. That is, as it were, the Church of God as something that is absolutely in the place of authority and government. That is the thing that these walls speak of. They speak of the conservation of all that has been recovered and restored.

Well, we have said that about the walls because otherwise we would have much to talk about when we come to these chapters which are all about the walls of Jerusalem. One other little point—Nehemiah comes in. He is another remarkable man. We cannot spend time speaking about Nehemiah now, but he was a remarkable man, one of the loveliest characters, I think, in the Old Testament, when you really look at him. There is something very lovely about his word and very lovely about his character. There is something very appealing about Nehemiah.

This also is the period of the prophecy and ministry of Malachi. We do not know how much Malachi is responsible for this part of the recovery. As Haggai and Zechariah, in the first stage of the recovery, were so greatly used of God to complete it, to bring about completion, it may well have been that Malachi was used by God to bring about the completion of these walls.

Deep, Inwrought Experience

What are the principles that we find here in Nehemiah? There are five clear principles in these thirteen chapters. (By the way, I trust you will bear in mind all that has preceded in the first and second stage of the return because the testimony of Jesus of course is that.) The first thing we find in Nehemiah 1—2:18 is this: holding the testimony of Jesus is a deeply inwrought matter. It requires a deep inwrought experience if there is to be any recovery of the testimony and any holding of the testimony.

The Spirit of Concern

Now just look at this man Nehemiah in chapter one. The first thing you find in him is the spirit of concern. There is a spirit of concern and exercise. This is nothing cheap here. It is not ambition, it is not ministry, it is not position, it is not just himself. This man has a spirit of concern. Although he occupied a very high position in the court, as soon as one of his close associates comes from the promised land he asks about the city. "What happened?" There is a spirit of real concern for the people of God. He is living actually in exile but his heart is in the land. His heart is where God's dwelling place is and he has a concern for it. Oh, here is a spirit of concern. It is nothing cheap. It is nothing superficial, nothing shallow, but a spirit of *real* concern.

The Spirit of Brokenness and Travail

You will see straight on in that chapter that there is a spirit of brokenness and travail. The reaction of Nehemiah is not just an emotional one. It is the reaction of an educated, cultured, refined man who is in deep travail of spirit. It is not just sentimentality. As soon as he hears the news, the affliction of the people of God and the breaking down of those walls, it says he wept. Now the trouble with so many of us is that when we hear of that which should not be, we rejoice. Or at the very least we just talk, we gossip instead of having a spirit of concern that would bring about tears. Here, Nehemiah has a spirit of brokenness and travail. If you read the tremendous prayer of Nehemiah, it bubbles out of the depths of this man. He cannot contain it. He cannot keep it in. This man is so deeply involved with God's purpose.

Holding the testimony of Jesus is really something that goes right down to our spirit. Now, I wonder whether any of you have ever wept over the work of God. This you can judge. I do not necessarily mean outwardly, but inwardly. Have any of you really wept over the interest of God? There are many of us who have wept over our own need. We spend a lot of time thinking about ourselves—whether we're loved or not loved or whether we're wanted or not wanted or whether we're careful or not careful and all the rest of it. I wonder if any of us have really ever had such a spirit of concern, such a spirit of exercise, such a spirit of humility and brokenness that draws out prayer. You cannot force prayer out. Prayer comes out! He cannot keep it in! This man is in such agony, the only way he can do it is let it out in prayer. Have you ever been like that? When there is only one way out and that is prayer. You have got to pray! Otherwise, you just cannot contain yourself any longer, you have got to pray it out!

Evidently, this man, was not usually of a sad countenance and the king very quickly noticed it. In those days a cupbearer could lose his head if his countenance was not happy. He feared for his life when the king said to him, "What is wrong with you, Nehemiah? You are not sick and yet your countenance has changed. There is something desperately wrong with you."

Utter Dependence Upon the Lord

This reveals the next thing. This man is utterly dependent upon the Lord. Before ever he answered the king, he said, I prayed, and the Lord led me. He only had a minute you know? He didn't bow his head and get on his knees; it was just in his heart. That revealed a spirit of dependence. Then, there is what we could call *action*—prayer in action. He asks for something. He takes his life in his hands and tells the king exactly what he requests.

If we are going to hold the testimony of Jesus or be any part to its recovery we have got to have an experience as this: a deeply inwrought experience of concern, of travail, of brokenness. Now, I do not wish to dwell much upon it, but you know when a person is in travail they know nothing else but that. It constrains them, and so it is in this. If we are going to be in this it is going be that one thing that is going to take us completely—a spirit of dependence.

A Practical Knowledge and Understanding

Fourthly, I also just want to add this: a practical knowledge and an understanding of the wall. I love the way that when Nehemiah went back to the city he went out by night. He went out on a donkey by night. He went right around the walls of the city. Now this is just what many Christians will not do and a lot of trouble comes from it. They think that it seems very critical to look at the ruins. If you clearly see the ruins and can say what the ruins are, there is something wrong with your sanctity. Or you are lacking in love. But the whole point is this: a surgeon has got to know what is wrong before he can operate. Before ever you can restore a building, you have got to know the extent of the rot.

When we came to Halford House[2] we did not just pretend that the building's damage did not exist but moved to find out where it was and *look* at it. We had to take in its full extent. I remember the horror of it when we realised, after taking in the full extent, just how far it had gone. We had to sit down and recognise that it was going to be a costly venture.

Now this is exactly what has got to be in all of us if there is going to be any recovery of the testimony. We have got to look at the state of things. We have got to review the ruins. We have got to see the rot. We have got to see the rubbish. We have got to see where it lies and what can be done about it. The first step in recovery is an understanding of the ruins.

---

2 Halford House in Richmond, England. For more of this story see Lance's testimony in "Let the House of God Be Built"

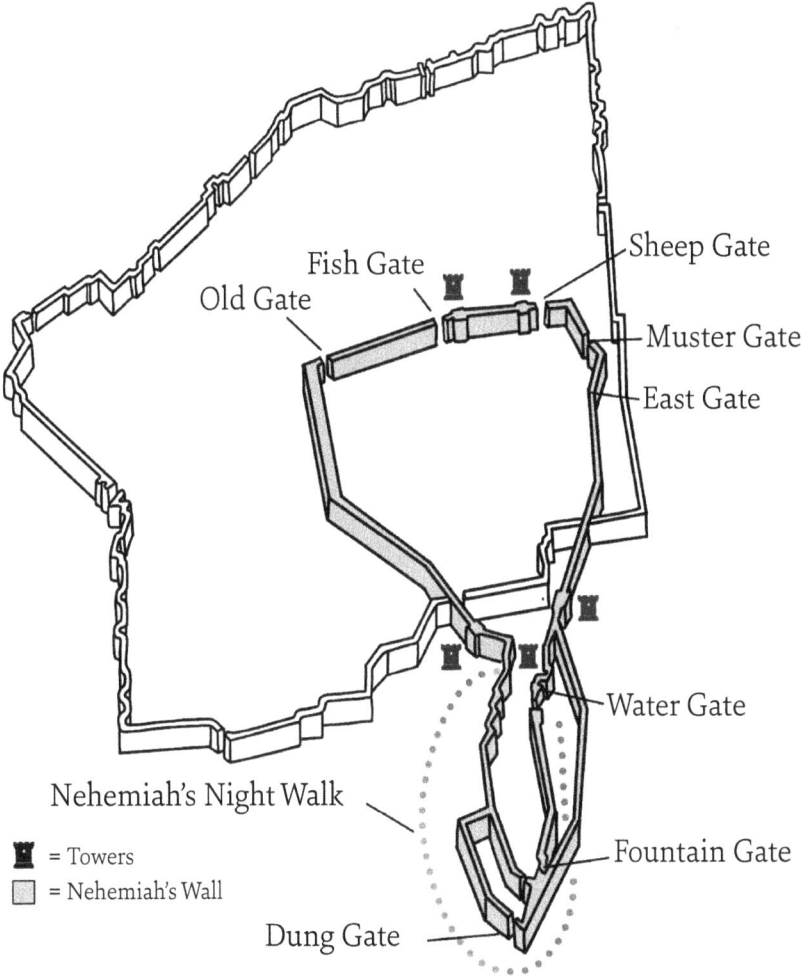

Old Gate

Fish Gate

Sheep Gate

Muster Gate

East Gate

Nehemiah's Night Walk

Water Gate

= Towers

= Nehemiah's Wall

Fountain Gate

Dung Gate

Of course, I do not mean these people that can throw their weight around, that can just, as it were, knock everyone about, and so on. That is not the spirit of brokenness and travail and dependence. When the Lord gets the spirit of brokenness and travail and dependence in us, then He can show us the ruins! First, He gets Nehemiah crying, then He shows him the ruins. When He gets that order, Nehemiah is safe. He won't throw his weight around. He can see the ruin, understand it, and in the hands of God he can be used to do something about it. God would have us like that—people in His hands, who could view the state of things today in Christian circles, and have the courage to define what is wrong. That is the thing that is needed. It needs courage to define what is wrong. It needs courage to see the rubbish, and it is rubbish, that locks up and blocks up—everywhere. But we need the courage, and we need the understanding and knowledge of such a thing before there can be any kind of recovery at all. If we are going to hold the testimony of Jesus, we are going to have to have an experience like that. *That* will take us in deep weather.

Fellowship, Harmony, and Relatedness of Function

Then if you move on, you will find another wonderful principle. The second principle is found in chapter three and chapter four. It is the necessity of fellowship, harmony, and relatedness of function in recovery of the testimony. Now, here there are some wonderful things if you have read these chapters. If you have not read them, you must read them, if you are going to get an understanding of what I am going to say.

Look at the harmony here. Look at the fellowship here. If we only had a map of the wall we could see right here one man and his group, and here another man and his group and next to him another man and his group, and next to him is another man and his group, and next to him is another man and his group. Then there is a leader for each section, over different groups, from group to group, you see? Then another leader over so many subsidiary groups and the whole thing is a marvel of the division of labour, all divided up carefully, right the way round the whole wall so that the walls go up slowly and together.

There are some wonderful things if you read through these chapters. Perhaps some of you find it a little bit much to read through all these things—the long names, and so-and-so, and so many, and the sheep gate and the horse gate and the dung gate and the fish gate and all the rest of it. However, if you read through it, what do you find? You find, here a goldsmith built, and then here there are perfumers. Here, there are merchants, and then here there are quite a gang of ordinary people and so, you go all the way around. You find the priests, you find the Levites, you find the rulers, and you even find one noble man and his very aristocratic daughters working on one of the gates. It is recorded very carefully, you see? Why is all this recorded so carefully? Because it reveals a marvel of interrelatedness. No one cared two hoots of their position. They might be the most aristocratic or the poorest person. They might be wealthy or they might be poverty stricken, but they all came in together. No one stood on their position; no one took knowledge of their craft. Everyone came together. In the recovery of the testimony, that is exactly how it must be—no social barriers, no other barriers. Everyone is equal in the sight of God. Everyone has a place on this wall. Everyone has to work beside each other.

Now, it is not that easy. I have no doubt at all that those aristocratic daughters of that noble man did not find it easy to be put beside some peasant people. I don't know. But I have no doubt at all that there were a lot of troubles on those walls if you could have gone all the way around between all the different people. They were all so different. Can you imagine?

Nehemiah says that the nobles of Tekoa, did not put their shoulders to the work. They evidently felt it was a bit beneath their dignity to so do. But, you see, this is a principle. It is a principle in the recovery of the testimony. It does not matter who you are, where you come from, what you are, how much money you have got, how much you have not got. The point is this: God requires you in the recovery of the testimony. He will put us all together in this business. All the different functions, all the different positions, all the different ministries are all there in this work of recovery. That is one thing that I wanted to say.

Then I want you also to note that each one is mentioned, each group is mentioned. It does not matter who they are or what they are. I am very glad to see that the rulers are given no bigger place than the ordinary people. Every one is the same. The priests do not get any different place than the rest, nor do the Levites. All are given the same place as far as mentioning goes. All are mentioned. This reveals that every part of those walls is as important to the completion of the walls. Do you see? It is very, very easy to think that the fish gate might be more important than an in between part of the wall. But in actual fact, one single breach in the wall, and that is the end of the safety of the land. There is no other way out. There must not be a weakness anywhere in those walls.

Now this is the testimony of Jesus. You might be the most humble person as far as job and background goes, but you are so necessary. You may feel you are so useless. You may wonder, "What do I do? I am so young, I am so small, I haven't very many spiritual riches," and the rest of it. But, you see, you and I, we are valuable in the Spirit. We have a part to play in the recovery.

I notice another thing that when some of them finish a little earlier than others they were re-dedicated to help finish the others. So that is a rather lovely thought, isn't it? When some got ahead of the others and finished their portion, they were given another portion to do, if you read through this list very carefully.

Then I want you also to note Nehemiah 4:7–23. The question of fellowship and relatedness of function in the recovery of the testimony goes right down to this question of vigilance and to fellowshipping vigilance and togetherness in defending. Oh, I do wish people would understand this simple lesson! You know this is just where the devil gets us all knocked out. Here you have got a tremendous work going on in recovery. It is all starting, working, as it were. The stones are all going into their place and slowly the walls are going up. Then what starts to happen? Well, so-and-so falls out with so-and-so. We can just imagine it. Perhaps the aristocratic ladies didn't like the people who were next to them. They just began to draw out of the work altogether. Difficulties ensued and arguments, collisions, and all the rest of it. It couldn't happen.

Nehemiah had to continually go around getting everyone together all the time. He said, "We have got to have a fellowship of vigilance. Everyone has got to watch over everyone else!" Those who are on duty, half are on duty, half are on guard. Then many who were on duty had a sword in one hand and a trowel in the other. "You have all got to guard one another. Everyone has got to watch." He said, "As the walls are rather big, if we see the enemy attacking over there, the trumpet will be blown and every man focus his attention on that part of the wall." No time for personal difficulties, no time for personal collisions, no time for the little squabbles that go on and cause ruin. It is the little foxes that spoil the vine. No time for these little things. It has got to be a fellowship in vigilance. A vigilant fellowship—all watching over each other, all helping one another, all covering each other, you see?

Oh, what do we do? Many of us are using our swords on one another. You have got a trowel in one hand and a sword in the other to dig the next person well and good when we get fed up with them. That is what is going on in the work all the time, these little sort of squabbles between people, but they are using their sword, they are using their weapon for the wrong thing. We need this fellowship in vigilance, this togetherness in defence. What a tremendous thing it is!

You know as well as I do, that one of the first things the enemy speaks is in order to sow disruption (that is why he has such a huge intelligence network). In the War, they tried to do it in the factories, they tried to do it in the homes, just sow disruption. Morale is one of the greatest factors in war. Smash up the morale and the fighting men can go on fighting. If you smash up the morale at home, it is gone. This is always the devil's weapon to try and get the morale of the people of God ruined. Ruined! He tries to destroy it, and he does it by people seeing faults in each other and all the rest of it, colliding and not covering each other, and so it goes on. Then of course when the trumpet is blown, everyone is so busy fighting each other or so full of despondency and despair that they say, "Oh, let the trumpet blow. I couldn't really care less."

Oh, to see the need, the necessity of fellowship and relatedness in function of the recovery of this testimony! You and I have a part to play as brothers. He has called us to cooperate in such a company that is returning. We have a very real part to play. Never underestimate your part. *Never*! You may seem very small. But it is a tremendous part and you might be the very one, if you let go, to cause a breach in the wall.

Conflict in the Recovery of the Testimony

Then I want you to note the third thing in this whole question, which is conflict and triumph in the recovery of the testimony. This is spread over quite a few chapters. In Nehemiah 2:19–20 and chapters four to six, you have this conflict. I am dealing with it all, as it were, together because I think it will help you to understand.

This conflict began with the commencement of the wall. It began with the commencement of the wall, and then it slowly went right on until the completion of the wall. It was a tremendous conflict. If we could only just see something of the nature of this conflict, we would be amazed.

The three leaders of the antagonism, of the opposition, are a man called Sanballat the Horonite, another man called

Tobiah the Ammonite, and the other man called Geshem, or Gashmu, the Arabian. Let us just take one small look at these three men. If you look into this book of Nehemiah you will be very, very interested to discover something about the background of these three. (At least two of them are more clear.)

Take for instance, Sanballat. Sanballat, as far as we know, was a very, very influential man indeed. He later became governor of Samaria. Indeed, Jewish tradition tells us that he built a temple. This is very interesting. He built a Samaritan temple on Mount Gerizim. Interesting. He not only did that, but he was a Moabite. Now, you all know that Moabites are descendants of Lot. You remember Lot, when he was drunk, had sons by his own daughters. One was the father of the Moabites; the other was the father of the Ammonites. Sanballat was a Moabite from Horonea—a Horonite. That is just very, very interesting. If you read very carefully in Nehemiah 13:28, you will find that this Sanballat's daughter married the high priest's grandson. There was an alliance, so it is not quite so simple as you would think. This man, Sanballat, was related to the high priest of all people, which did not make it very easy for Nehemiah. His daughter married the grandson of the high priest. Now, that just shows you the mix-up there. A very, very influential man, Sanballat. He had a standing army. If you look into it, you will see that he speaks at one point of his army and rousing up the people of Samaria. A very interesting man.

Then Tobiah, who is Tobiah? Well, if you look at Tobiah, his name means the *Lord is Good, Jehovah is good.* That is his name and evidently he has got some very close associations with the Lord's people. Nevertheless, he is an Ammonite, another one of the descendants of Lot. A very interesting man. If we look into it, we find Tobiah is very, very popular. He is not just influential in power, he is popular. Many of the noblemen, the aristocrats, of Jerusalem and so on had a very real affinity to Tobiah. At one point Tobiah lived in the temple. (A little farther on we shall find that Nehemiah turned him out.) He was actually living in one of the chambers of the house of God. That shows you that this man was absolutely in the inner circle of the leaders of the nation. Tobiah. Again, I am afraid to say that he was related to nearly everyone. We find in one place that it says that the high priest had an alliance with Tobiah. None of us know what the alliance is but it is very interesting to see that he had a son that married a Jewish girl, a Levite's daughter, and Tobiah himself had married a Jewish woman. So, now you see two leaders of the opposition.

The third is a man called Geshem or Gashmu. We do not know so much about this man, but he is evidently very influential because when Sanballat writes he says then, "Geshem sent me." So, evidently what Geshem says is very, very important. Geshem is an Arabian, and Arabians are the descendants of the Edomites, that is, their father was Esau.

So, now we have a most interesting thing. We have an opposition that all find their origins somewhere amongst the people of God. And they are not only so, but they are all well related to the people of God. They have either got Jewish wives, or Jewish sons-in-law, or Jewish daughters-in-law and so on. They are all very closely related to the people of God. Now, get that in the background and now let's look.

Attempts to Stop the Work

First of all, if we look at Nehemiah 2:19—20, we have the first great attempt to stop the walls. It says the three of them, Sanballat, Tobiah, and Geshem, "They laughed us to scorn and despised us and said, What is this thing that ye do?" Their first attempt was laughter. They laughed. There is nothing so hard to bear as laughter. Nothing.

Can you imagine it? Here was Nehemiah, and here was this handful of willing men and here were these strong people round about, already planted in the land. As far as they were concerned the land was theirs, not Nehemiah's and his company. And of course, the first thing they did was to just make it a joke. "Goodness gracious, these most stupid people." (You know that kind of laughter.) "Who do they think they are? Do they really think that they, that little group, have got something? Do they think they have seen something? Well, surely, if they have seen, then we would have all seen it. How come they have seen it but we have not seen it?" It was that kind of laughter and derision. *Scorn.* Scorn is a terrible thing to put up with, but the hardest thing to put up with is that kind of scorn.

Well, that is how it began, in a very small way, this opposition. It always does. This opposition always begins with scorn. It usually begins just like that.

Nehemiah's reaction is very, very wonderful. He said, "The God of heaven, He will prosper us. Therefore, we His servants will arise and build. But ye have no portion with us," (see Nehemiah 2:20). That is the reaction.

Of course that set the tone. Sanballat, Tobiah, and Geshem are now enemies. I have no doubt about it that if dear old Nehemiah had opened his arms wide and said, "Come on, boys. Come and help. Let's all be friends together," it would have made the greatest difference in the world, but he had no portion with them. He could not. They are going to cause trouble. They will cause trouble in the end.

Anger and Scorn

That meant they were enemies and very soon we find the next great attempt. In Nehemiah 4:1—6 we find it is anger and scorn this time. When they heard that the walls were begun, they were angry! We find a slightly different language that takes place. They say, "What are these feeble Jews doing? Will they fortify themselves? Will they sacrifice?" Then Tobiah adds his little three cents, and he says, "Even a fox could push down their stone wall!" You know that kind of talk; they were angry now. Something was happening and they knew it. Something was happening.

Then they pour scorn on it. "Just give them time, give them time. They'll flag. [Become unsteady, feeble, or spiritless]." You find that Nehemiah's reaction in 4:4—6 is one of dependence. He turns to the Lord; he won't answer them. This is the point we have got to notice. Nehemiah refuses to take them on; he won't answer them. He only answers the minimum, when he has to. He always turns to the Lord and he pours it all out before the Lord. He says, "Now, Lord, You listen to that. Hear what they say? They say a fox could push down this wall."

Antagonism in Action

Then you go on to the third great attempt in Nehemiah 4:7—14. It is definite antagonism in action. Now, what do Sanballat, and Tobiah, and Geshem do? They decide that, by means of an insidious propaganda, they are going to divide and bring about disintegration within. So, they start the ball rolling, as it were, with all kinds of rumours; you can just imagine it. Later on they come out into the open with little things like: "Nehemiah wants to be king. This is all for Nehemiah. It all centres on Nehemiah. Nehemiah is everything. Nehemiah wants this city for himself."

Those kinds of things are the things that cause trouble because if there is any ground of doubt in the people, they will listen. Once they start to listen, then the snowball begins to grow. But Nehemiah's reaction is one of very real interest; it is very, very interesting. He arms everyone. He realises that real attacks are coming, so now everyone is vigilant. He answers by fellowship. It is not just himself. He seeks for everyone to be together in this work, and really quietly, not to stop the work. They go right on with the work, but being vigilant; all the time together in the defence and not stopping. You see all these attempts are to stop the walls. Stop the walls. Anything, to stop those walls from being built. You must not stop the walls.

Opposition from Within

Then, if you go on you find that the fourth opposition is from within. Now, this time it was not Sanballat, nor was it Tobiah. It is entirely different. This time it was from within. I am afraid that this wonderful harmony and fellowship is broken down, and the noble people have been very swiftly buying up the land of the poor people. What happened was this: the poor people who came to build the wall, left their land, and because of that, they hadn't any food. So they mortgaged their land and the rich people with the money started to buy up all the land they could get from their poor brothers and sisters. The result was that these people in the end having eaten to the full, found that now they had neither any land to mortgage or homes or furniture or anything to mortgage and no money to buy any more food! So division came from within.

This had nothing to do with Sanballat. It came from right within. This time it was dishonesty and greed; it was selfishness inside the wall. This again and again has brought to an end the work of God. Oh, it can happen in so many ways. Just get a company of people all centering in on their own things and the work immediately stops at that point.

They had to be put right and the way it was put right is only one. Nehemiah took some very strong action and gets all the land given back by the wealthier people, but he also tells them that he himself has never taken a penny from anyone and neither will he. Although he's governor and he's entitled to take quite a bit from them, he says he is not going to take any money at all from these people. That is an answer of fellowship. Real fellowship. That was the only way through really, the only way through.

An Insidious and Subtle Attempt

Then, you will find that a very interesting attempt came in Nehemiah 6. This was perhaps the most insidious and subtle attempt of all. "Come and have a conference with us." Now, Sanballat and Geshem and Tobiah said, "If you could only have a round table conference to put all these things right, we will all be happy. Come to this little village on the plain of Ono and there we will have this round table conference."

However, Nehemiah said that he was doing too great of work to come down. That was his only argument. You see the thing that was concerning Nehemiah was the walls. He was a discerning man. He knew very well that there was no real desire, really. Even though they pleaded for this thing, there was no real desire. He may well have known that there was no possibility of it going on, of it being put right because of their mixed background, particularly in history. He would not come down. Four times they asked for this conference. Four times he answered exactly the same.

Another Attempt to Stop the Work

And then we come to the next attempt. This time it is a letter. Now letters can be terrible things and Sanballat sends a letter that was full of charges. Sanballat was very clever. He never said that he was charging Nehemiah. These people who write letters never do. He never made the charges himself. All he simply said was, "It has been said that *you* want to be king, that you have appointed prophets to talk about you, and that you intend to take the kingdom for yourself." That is all. He says, "Furthermore, Geshem said it. It has been heard among the nations and Geshem said it."

Evidently, you can be absolutely definite that this was a very serious matter indeed. For the first time Nehemiah answered the charge. He says, "You have feigned the whole thing." That is all. He makes his appeal to the Lord for strengthening.

The Seventh Attempt to Stop the Work

Then I think the next attempt, the seventh attempt was the most insidious of all. It was a very, very clever one indeed. A man who was a very good man evidently, and had a ministry—he was a prophet—came to Nehemiah and said, evidently, "Tonight there is going to be an attempt on your life. You come with me and we will hide in the temple."

Now Nehemiah was not a priest, not like Ezra. He knew that it was forbidden by God for anyone except the priests and Levites to enter into the Tent of Meeting. The attempt here was to get Nehemiah to fear for his own life and to hide in the place where they would not dream of looking for him and where they would not be allowed to go, and he would be safe. But they knew very well that the moment he did that, he was finished because he would be stoned to death. They would have their first well-grounded charge to make against him: that he had stepped foot within the temple of God. No man would be allowed to do that and live.

Nehemiah saw through that and he said that he was not the kind of man to flee. "Why should such a man as I flee?" he said. Then he makes his appeal to the Lord. And so it says in chapter 6:15: "So the wall was finished." Now, that is the conflict for you.

Triumph

Of course, I have been most impolite and interpreted it all in practical terms, to get down to brass tacks as it were. But you know, this is the kind of thing that happens again and again and again in every part of the work of God. You can see the strategy of the enemy—I am not blaming the people. I am blaming the enemy. The enemy has a strategy and he uses people like pawns in this strategy, backwards and forwards and over—anything, anything, anything—but with one great object to stop the work. Stop the walls from being built. Stop the completion of the walls. Stop the testimony of Jesus from being recovered. He uses anything to stop it. Wreck the unity! Throw out this integration! Rupture the thing! Do anything to stop the wall. Nehemiah was a man that was apprehended of God. The one thing that governed him from beginning to end in this conflict was that whatever happened, the walls were not stopping.

It is interesting when you look through that you find that at each point it mentions how far the walls are up. They were halfway up and a new attack began and a little bit further up, and so it went on. Till at last the walls were finished and the battle was not over even then!

The Last Attempt

The last attempt was this: many of the nobles sent letters to Tobiah, and Tobiah sent letters to the nobles. Then these noble people came to Nehemiah and told of Tobiah's good deeds. Well they may well be—Tobiah was evidently a good man. There were a lot of good deeds about Tobiah. Of course I suppose it was very difficult for poor Nehemiah to sit down and hear that Tobiah was a very good man. He did this for so-and-so, he did that for so-and-so, and on and on. He must be right. So it says that Tobiah sent letters that made Nehemiah fear as an attempt to stop the walls. But there is a triumph there; you see the walls never stopped. That is the point. That is the principle. There is a triumph.

Commit to the Lord

Now what is the principle? The principle is that in the recovery of the testimony we must expect the enemy to come at us from every angle! He will come at us outside. He will come at us from within sometimes. Those of us who are the most godly, the most spiritual, and the most responsible will probably at some point become the enemy's tools. Perhaps only for a month. That sometimes happens. The principle is this: never take anything on. Never. If you know in your spirit that the aim is to bring us down here turn these people in on themselves, get them all talking, get them all, as it were, centred in on what they are and what they are not and all the rest of it. Oh, the walls stop. You do not have to worry about the walls.

The principle is this: every time Nehemiah committed it to the Lord. I am not saying that Nehemiah said every time he was right in what he did each time. He said, "Lord, you see this thing. See?" I don't know when he heard about the fox pushing down the stonewall. He said, "Well, now Lord, hear them. Hear what they say." He did not say, "Oh, a fox can't do it, Lord." He just said, "You listen to them, Lord." In other words he was saying, "Lord, they are taking You on with these things they say."

Oh, these kinds of things are going on all the time. Whenever you have got any who are going back, (a remnant returning) who are going on in this business, in a vanguard of recovery, you have got this stupid talk. But you have got to remember that in every single move of recovery, from the day of Hus or of Luther or Fox, right down to this day, every single move has had scorn heaped upon it. Derision is heaped upon it and it is being laughed at. "Who do these people think that they are?" What were the Methodists called? They were called Methodists, "new fangled religionists." That is what they were called in the press of the day. What was the great Brethren movement called? Even Spurgeon called them poor, hobnobbing, clutterbucks.

Now, let's take Erasmus. There was no greater, more learned, more gentle, more gracious Christian man, and yet he *heaped* scorn upon Luther. He was Luther's greatest antagonist. Of course, a lot that Erasmus said was true about Luther. We know the poor bishop would admit saying so—the pope was the antichrist and many other things like that. Erasmus pointed those things out. Do you see? Scorn has been poured upon every move of the Holy Spirit until it is completed. Once concluded, then of course, these people all sit down and write history books. Then they say, "This was a great move of the Holy Spirit." However, the point is this: God was in a movement of recovery.

5.
The Return under Nehemiah & the Testimony of Jesus

We come now to the third stage of the return to the Land from the captivity. We have previously reviewed two stages of the return to the land from the book of Ezra. You will remember very simply that the first return was all to do with what we call the recovery of truth in practice, not merely doctrine, but truth in practice. There is a realm of reality. There is a ground of reality. There is a ground of truth. The first thing God had foreshowed, or typified, in the return to the land was the recovery of that ground, the getting back of that ground, the getting back of that realm. We call it the house of God.

You remember that first return under Zerubbabel was all to do with the recovery of the house of God. It was a question of being such as ground. It is a question of such a thing as the altar, and of the foundation, and of the completion of the house. Those are all fundamental things to do with a realm. All those things which are absolutely necessary, in an elementary way, if the Lord's purpose is going to be secured. He has to have a people on a certain ground. No matter how few, they have to be on a certain ground. When He has them on a certain ground, there has to be the cross working in them. When the cross works in them, a foundation is laid on which something can be built. That foundation is just an essential experience of the oneness and life of Christ. Then the house is built.

The second return, about 70 years later, was led by Ezra and was much smaller in number. It had nothing to do with building. The building of the walls is hardly mentioned; I believe it is mentioned once in these four chapters. Building and the rebuilding and recovery of the house of God is hardly mentioned again. It is all to do with the recovery of inward, spiritual character—moral character. Everything in those chapters, from Ezra 7—10, is all to do with inward character. You remember Ezra and his great drive, his great cry to the people, and everything to do with it. Every part of those chapters is to do with the question of that inward character.

Then we pointed out the order of the Holy Spirit. First, the recovery of truth in practice, then the recovery of inward spiritual character. We asked you to note the present day inversion of that order by modern Christianity. Today, it is all a question of inward spiritual character. Every conference, every convocation, every convention—all these things have one aim: to produce spiritual character in the people of God. The aim of many other great societies and organisations is to produce spiritual character. This is all commendable. This is something that we would all commend very greatly, we have no quarrel with it, even though many people do think we have got a quarrel with it. But when it comes down to practice, the place where we cannot, as it were, "toe the line," where we cannot fall in with it, where we cannot cooperate with it is simply this: the whole order is inverted. To put it crudely, the cart is put before the horse. The Holy Spirit puts the question of a realm first, and then the question of spiritual character. To us, this may not seem right because of the way we have been conditioned into thinking, rightly in some ways, that spirituality is the key to everything. This is true. Spirituality or godliness, is to our gain wherever it is, but it is not to the gain of God. Spirituality in us is only to God's gain when we are on certain ground. Therefore, this two-fold book puts it so clearly.

First, it is no good having spiritual people in exile as far as the Lord is concerned. It is all right for them. Thank God for Esther! Thank God for Mordecai! Thank God for those spiritual people in exile! They saved their countrymen, but it was of no great account to God that Mordecai lived or Esther. It did not in any way vitally affect His purpose whether they lived or whether they died, whether they were righteous or whether they were unrighteous. Terrible as it may seem, it did not in any way vitally affect God's purpose because they were not on the right ground. But let God have one man called Zerubbabel and a few others joined to him on the right ground, and God's purpose is immediately set in motion. Everything starts. Immediately, as it were, all the great wheels of the machinery of God start to move because He's got a few people—poor, simple, wayward people, but they are on the right ground. When He has got them on the right ground, He can start to do something.

So He gets them back to Jerusalem, He starts them with an altar built, then He gets a foundation and then we have a house. Then He starts on inward character. Now, this is the order that present day Christianity has completely inverted, so that you have got all this great activity to save people, and all this great activity to sanctify people, and what really is the outcome? So much money, so much energy, so much activity, so much work, for what?

You had twelve people at Ephesus, twelve poor, almost benighted, people in Ephesus. The Holy Spirit comes on them and one of the finest churches of the New Testament develops overnight. That is what happens when you get a few people on the right ground. All God's machinery starts to operate. It starts into motion. Do you see?

Oh, it may seem so critical to some people, but you know that if the surgeon is going to get anywhere, he has to be pretty definite. He must not blunder. He must not just cut you up anywhere. He has got to know where he is going to operate. He has got to know what the condition is. He must have a correct diagnosis.

We have a terrible, terrible situation that faces us today. The situation is a very simple one. It is not being stupid or maliciously critical to point it out, to say this: that in all the years of convention ministry and gatherings there have been, there has not been produced one church like Ephesus. Anywhere. Not one place like Ephesus has been produced anywhere by all of those years of conference and convention work. Now, that is the kind of thing that should make us all sit up and reflect. Is the Holy Spirit the same? Is the purpose of God the same? If it is, then there is something wrong somewhere. I would suggest that what is wrong is the inversion of an order, that it does not matter *where* you have spirituality so long as you *have* spirituality. You can belong to anything, you can be anywhere, you can live anywhere and all the rest of it, so long as you are spiritual.

Well, the first two stages of the return that comprise the book of Ezra clearly teach us that, first of all, the first thing is to get a realm clear. Now don't any of you get me wrong. I have not said that spirituality is wrong and I have not said spirituality is not a vital necessity. Neither have I even said that spirituality is not gain. But I have said this: that spirituality is no gain, or of any real value to God when it is off His ground. It is to our gain. Godliness will always be to our gain—wherever we are. God will always commend it. But it is of no intimate, direct value to Himself when it is off that ground. He cannot do anything with it. He has certain ground.

You have the whole Old Testament; the Lord says to them again and again you cannot offer your burnt offering just anywhere. You cannot bring your heave offering or your tithe or anything else just anywhere. If you do, I will not accept them. There may be a lot of good motive and that is fine, but I will not accept them. There is only one place I will accept it, the place where I will cause my name to dwell. You come there and I will accept everything you bring there. I will accept you in person there.

The Third Stage of the Return

Now we come to the third stage of the return. When we come to the third stage, which followed approximately twelve years after the second stage, we find that it was led by Nehemiah and that it was probably an even smaller number than the company that returned under the leadership of Ezra. The whole of Nehemiah speaks, really, of the wall. It is comprehended by the wall. In reviewing what we learned, you will remember that I told you that the first seven chapters of Nehemiah deal almost exclusively with the wall. The whole of the first seven chapters centre in the walls of Jerusalem being rebuilt. The twelfth chapter of Nehemiah, is dealing almost completely with the dedication of the walls. Then come those other chapters, the last part of chapter seven, eight, nine, ten, and eleven—and here is the interesting point: those chapters are dealing with inward character again. Now, mark that very, very carefully because this time it intertwines.

In the first return, everything was to do with the house of God. There was no talk about character at all. It was all to do with the house of God. Everything to do with it: the ground, the altar, the foundation, and then the actual house being built and completed upon it. In the second return they hardly refer to the building, twice only is it referred to. It is all to do with character, purity of character. When we come to Nehemiah, the third return, we find the house of God and inward character completely intertwined. That is, what the Holy Spirit has sought so clearly to define in the first two stages of the return are now brought together completely. That is very important for us to understand.

In the third return we are dealing with something much more full than the previous two stages. What do the walls really symbolise? Now, we are going to spend time on this because I want not just to review it, but I also want to add what I feel to be a very vital note to what we last said on these chapters. (I am quite sure now when we look back, this is probably the reason why we have had to leave the whole thing for a month or more.) What do these walls really symbolise? It is obviously of tremendous importance. What do they symbolise? All these chapters are taken up with rebuilding some walls. What do they really symbolise? Now, we find that they speak of a city enclosed. This city which is enclosed by these walls is the hub, or to put another way, at the hub of this city is the house of God and the city itself is the heart of the people, of a nation.

Immediately, you have got those two things again. Do you see? You have got the first stage and the second stage immediately intertwined. This is the interesting part: these walls, when they were actually built, were built around a more or less uninhabited city. The strange and impressive thing is that the actual houses, according to this book, were built later. The walls were built first. But at the very heart of the city, as the walls went up, was the house of God; it was there. All its services were in progress. Everything was functioning. This city not only had as its hub, the house of God, the dwelling place of God, but the city itself was the metropolis of the nation. It was going to be the heart of the nation. *The* main artery of the whole nation was this city. Now, the walls enclose that.

The Purpose of the Walls

We said, if I remember rightly, that these walls speak of three things. They speak of definition, separation, and preservation. Of course, those three things obviously overlap. They speak of definition, separation, and preservation. That is, what has been recovered is defined clearly by those walls. Certain ground, and everything recovered within that ground and on that ground, is now walled so that it is clearly and forever defined. The boundaries are marked.

It is not only clearly defined but it is separated, that is, it is kept pure by those walls. Not just anything can enter. There are certain gates that can be watched, and they were watched, they were guarded. In this book, we find that one of the things that Nehemiah does is to set guards, day and night, over those few gates into the city. The whole idea was to keep the city pure. Separation, all those walls speak of separation. Something kept pure. Something separated. Not only defined but separated from the rest. You cannot mix it up with anything else. It has now been separated into an entity.

Then the last thing is preservation. Those walls preserve something. They are for protection. They are to ensure security. Those walls are for preservation. That means simply that all that has been recovered is now conserved.

Thus we find that these walls speak of a city that is enclosed and this gathers up all the characteristics of the other two stages into one. It now, as it were, flings a boundary, flings a wall around the lot. It bounds them and says: everything now is symbolised within these walls. This city is not only the ground of the dwelling place of God, but this city is the leading place in this nation. It is the example of the nation. It is the showplace of the nation. It is the type of the nation. The character here exemplified is really the character of the nation. That is why prophets often refer to the people of Jerusalem symbolising the whole nation in its capital, Jerusalem.

The Walls and the Testimony of Jesus

You will well remember that we went one step further, and this is the part I want to stay on. We said that these walls really symbolise what we now call in the New Testament "the testimony of Jesus." We often use this phrase, the testimony of Jesus, but what do we mean, really, by the testimony of Jesus? I wonder if you would ask yourselves, quietly and privately, "What really is the testimony of Jesus?" I wonder, what you would say? How really you would answer that question? These walls symbolise the testimony of Jesus. What is this testimony?

I will say one thing about it before we actually answer the question. The testimony of Jesus is vested in or held by those that have all the characteristics of those two previous stages. The testimony of Jesus cannot be held just by anything or anyone. It is only entrusted when there are certain elementary and basic conditions fulfilled. It does not follow, by any means, that every Christian holds the testimony of Jesus. Far from it. The very fact that the Lord could speak of the candlestick being removed is an eloquent witness to the simple fact that thousands of his people may well not have that candlestick in their midst. They may not hold or bear the testimony of Jesus.

What is the testimony of Jesus? These walls symbolise the testimony of Jesus. And these walls gather up all that has preceded.

The Testimony the Lord Jesus Bore

What is the testimony of Jesus? Well, let us put it as simply as we can. Christ, when He came into this world, bore testimony to God. It was just as if for the first time in abject darkness, a light shone in and when that light shone in, it showed up every kind of filth, degradation, depravity, and deception. When you go into a gloomy room, you don't know how really filthy it is, until suddenly, either the sun bursts into that room or you bring really powerful light into it. Then, like the heart in gloom, you realise the condition that room was in. This world was just like that.

When Christ came into this world it was just as if a tremendous light shone into this world for the first time. It had shone dimly through the prophets and through the people of God down through succeeding generations, but when the Lord Jesus came, it was just as if the light of God flooded into this world. When the light of God flooded into this world, for the first time, man saw himself as he really was and saw himself as the deception that he had become. It is absolutely true that wherever the Lord Jesus went in His life, He was showing up something all the time. It was as if men and women were deceived by life, absolutely deceived, and had no idea of the deception that they were living in. They suddenly touched Him and He suddenly touched them and immediately the whole deception fell off. It was as if they saw for the first time what a deception this life is. They saw that the whole thing originated in a lie. It was built on a lie. It was maintained by a lie.

Wherever the Lord Jesus went, the Lord Jesus was the presence of God. Wherever He went He exposed situations, He exposed the deceptions. It does not matter who it is—the woman taken in adultery, or Lazarus when he died, or a man, paralytic for many years, or someone born blind, or something else. People had all their deceived ideas about the sin of their parents, and the sin of this man, or something else exposed. But when the Lord Jesus came into the situation the whole thing simply fell away and people saw the truth. That was the testimony Jesus bore. He bore a testimony. Wherever He went He testified to the truth, to reality. Do you see? He testified to it. He speaks of Himself in the Scripture as the light of the world. He says that whoever comes to Him shall be given light. He speaks of men being afraid to come to the light, lest their deeds, being evil, shall be discovered as such. Men will prefer to stay in the shadows where they can live in the deception. But once they come out into the searchlight of Christ, then what is evil is shown up to be evil, what is sin is shown up to be sin, and the end of it all is clearly set forth. That is the testimony Jesus bore.

The Lord Jesus as the Testimony

However, the Lord Jesus did not only bear the testimony, the Lord Jesus was in Himself the testimony. It was not only that He pointed to God and revealed and manifested to man in His life, in His preaching, in His ministry, what God was like and who God was; it was much more than that. The Lord Jesus was Himself the testimony in that He was, in one being, God and man. He revealed to man, God as God really is. When He wept it was God. When He loved it was God. God was in Christ, reconciling man. Whenever man looked on Christ, they were looking on God. This is what God is like. Not the caricature you have always believed from childhood. Not that fallacy. *This* is God. So that whenever men and women touched Jesus, they touched God. God incarnate. God in the flesh. God living amongst men. Always He brought Him into view. Always. He was in Himself God. It was not only that, He was, in Himself, man. So that whenever man looked at the Lord Jesus, they saw Him as the man God intended them to be. You see the Lord Jesus not only *bears* the testimony, He *is* the testimony. Thereafter, it is simply referred to in Scripture as the testimony of Jesus—a lovely, simple term of the greatest fact of all. That is all. The key to His birth, the key to His life, the key to His ministry, the key to His death, the key to His resurrection— the testimony of Jesus.

The Candlestick of Pure Gold

Now, that testimony is vested or held by the church expressed on earth alone. It is not held by individuals. It is held, it is vested in, it is entrusted to the church as it is expressed on earth. It is spoken of always as that candlestick of pure gold. Now you see this candlestick of pure gold is found in the midst of people in their different localities according to John. There it is: the church of Ephesus, the church at Laodicea, the church at Smyrna, the church at Thyatira, the church somewhere else. In the midst of each one, is the candlestick of pure gold, one beaten piece. The testimony of Jesus is entrusted to the church of God as expressed in time, in place and in locality on earth. That is the testimony of Jesus.

When the Lord Jesus went to glory, when He was exalted to the right hand of God, the Holy Spirit was given and the church was born. That was the moment that the testimony of Jesus was entrusted into the hands of the members of Christ. Do you understand? His testimony, which had up to then been a personal matter, Himself, was now by the Holy Spirit put into the hands of His body on earth. It was therefore from the very beginning a matter to do with the body. It is a church matter. A body matter, or however you like to describe it. It was something to do with the church only. The book of Acts, as you well know and have often heard, is only the record of the triumph of that testimony through the body of the Lord Jesus. What the Lord Jesus began both to do and to preach personally, the book of Acts takes up corporately. He went on teaching and doing things through His body. The testimony continues.

What is His testimony? Well, don't you see? The whole point of this testimony is that we should be here on this earth, exactly what the Lord Jesus was on this earth. Wherever the church goes, this world should be exposed. Whatever the church touches in situations, any deception should be shown up. Wherever the church, as it were, is brought in on something, light shines in. The Lord Jesus said, "I am the light of the world," and "*Ye* are the light of the world!" He spoke of the church as a lampstand with seven branches. Full light! What is this light for? This church is not something in itself, it is only the body of Jesus. It is just the light—now through a body. Not anymore in one person, but through His body. The head is in the glory, the body is on earth. We are not talking about that part of the church which has gone to the glory, we are talking about the church in its earthly expression. Do you see?

The Purpose of the Church

Now the whole point of the church at present in its earthly expression is that it should be the continuation of the ministry and the life of Jesus. That is all. Now do you begin to see something of why we are always emphasising the church? It is because it is absolutely essential. All around you everywhere, you have got men and women living in the shadows, living in the gloom. It is no good hammering at them. It is no good cursing them. It is no good just shuttling them out, bypassing them. These people have not, as yet, had the light shine in. You see? The only way the light can really shine in is through the members of Christ, His body.

Oh, it should be just the same story! I'm sure of it! If we read the book of Acts, it is meant to say to us, "Look here! All that the Lord Jesus did when He was here has not ended with Calvary! It is to go on; it is one glorious story!" That woman in adultery, there should be many of them *here*. People that have been paralysed in sin. People who are blind. People who are lame and so we could go on. What do all of these people need? They do not need religious gatherings. They do not even really want religious campaigning. What they want is the testimony of Jesus. If they could only touch reality. If they could somehow reach out in this world to find something that was like a beacon. Something that did not just talk to them, but something that revealed something. Something that did not just preach to them in an evangelistic way, but something that expressed His life. People are in the habit of seeing through all this other stuff so often, just seeing right through it all. They do not know why, but it does not ring a bell.

Now, the testimony of Jesus is just simply *that life* now in a people and that life has a light. There is a light in that life and wherever that light touches, it brings life. Whenever people come into it, suddenly the deception in which they have lived, the lies that have been borne in show up for what they are. They begin to see: "I've lived a lie! I am in my own self a lie."

That is the testimony of Jesus, and the devil knows it. He doesn't mind if you have spiritual individuals here and spiritual individuals there. He doesn't mind if you have groups of Christians here, and groups of Christians there. The Lord will use them. However, you get a few paltry, frail saints, and get them on the right ground and you start to see the cross working in those lives, the total cost of it all being worked out, and you begin to see an inward character being produced. The devil works himself up into a frenzy—anything to smash that production out of existence. He will smash that character building out of existence! He cannot leave it for a moment too long. He knows that it is like a bell tolling, ringing out his own end every moment that it exists longer; something tolling out the end. The devil will fight to stop that happening by every lie, insinuation, and device that can be brought to bear upon it. He will do it and then he has wrecked it. Absolutely wrecked it.

You see, this whole question of the testimony of Jesus, as we have said, is symbolised by these walls. But what do these walls mean? They have gathered up and have enclosed within themselves all that has been defined in the previous two stages of the return. Therefore, we understand that the testimony of Jesus can only be entrusted when we have all those characteristics functioning. That is, we have got to have a right ground, we have got to have a realm, we have got to know a group on that ground. We have got to know something of the cross. We have got to have an essential experience of Christ as our unity and life, in an elementary way. Then we have got to know something of an inward character. Consider the state of affection, of lies, and everything else. Getting right down to the root of the matter in each one individually. The other point has to do with getting a people in, getting a people onto that ground. Now, the next thing to do is to sort them all out; one by one, sort them all out. Get right down to this business of themselves—their affections, their feelings. That is where they stand, but first, get them on the ground.

Now are you beginning to get it? This testimony of Jesus then, we find in the New Testament, is not entrusted to individuals as individuals. It is not a question of spirituality, of spiritual individuals. Do you understand? It is not a question of spiritual individuals! It is not a question of an individual ministry. Nor is the testimony of Jesus given to groups, however spiritual. They may be the most spiritual group in this world, but they do not have the testimony of Jesus. It is not a question of the group. It is not even a question of corporate ministry. Some group has got the idea that the testimony of Jesus is a corporate ministry. It is not a question of a corporate ministry. The testimony of Jesus is found in people who are children of God gathered into Christ in their own locality and being built together by the work of the cross through the Holy Spirit. When you get that, however poor, however sinful, however seamy it is, the testimony of Jesus is there. You can have a Jezebel there. You can have much else that is called adultery there, but you do have the candlestick there. That may have to be dealt with, and it *will* be dealt with, but it is an eloquent reminder that they are not all holy, holy places who have got hold of a great deal of the truth, but are excluding everyone else. Evidently, they cannot turn anyone out who is a child of God. They find that they have got to stay together and they have got to overcome *there*. You do not overcome by leaving and starting something else. You overcome by staying on the ground that God gives you.

But, of course, there is another involved subject: that is that the candlestick can be taken away. Of course, how we know that the candlestick can be taken away is another very, very involved matter that we cannot deal with now. But the whole point is this: the testimony of Jesus is entrusted, you see, to *those* people on *that* ground. You have only got to read the first three chapters of the book of Revelation and you will discover just that simple fact. You will be horrified, I am quite sure, if you read it without your religious glasses on. You just read it as plain English, preferably in the Phillips version or something like that. It is not that I commend it unquestionably, but because I think it will bring home to you the heart of what you read—where this candlestick is found. You have got the ground and you have got a people on the ground. Then you have got the testimony of Jesus within those people—of course they are all born again believers. We know that. On that ground the testimony is kept. Everything is being judged in the light of that testimony. The whole book of Revelation is the story of the testimony of Jesus.

Whilst I have said it cannot be held by individuals, as individuals—this is perfectly true—it can be held by individuals as they are related to that body. If you read carefully, you will find you have someone like John. He speaks of himself as holding the testimony of Jesus and being on the island of Patmos for the testimony of Jesus. Individual. He cannot be gathering with the church on the isle of Patmos. He is down in the copper mines, gradually being worked to death. But you see the point is that he is there for the testimony of Jesus. Something happened to him in the mine. He was fused into something. He was built into something down there.

The Recovery of the Testimony of Jesus

We see therefore that this question upon which the whole book of Nehemiah dwells is a question of the recovery of the testimony of Jesus. Well, what does this mean? It means simply that if we are going to know in our day something of the recovery of that testimony, we have got to start where the Holy Spirit starts and we must not invert the order. We must observe the order. We study these books of Ezra and Nehemiah and we shall discover the order clearly enough. The testimony of Jesus. Let us make that abundantly clear. You could have a people on the right ground, you could have a people that might have all the pattern and they might have all the knowledge and everything else, but the testimony might not be there. The testimony of Jesus is not only a question of the recovery of truth in practice, but it is a question of inward spiritual character. It is two things woven together, two things that the Holy Spirit has kept distinctly apart in the book of Ezra, now fused together. That is the testimony of Jesus.

The Spirit of Travail and Discernment

Very simply, looking at Nehemiah—and this is a review—we have found, three things about the recovery of the testimony of Jesus. The first thing we found was this: there has got to be a very real experience of travail and a very practical knowledge of the ruins if the testimony of Jesus is going to be recovered. Remember? Now, look at the first chapters of Nehemiah. The first chapter is almost all taken up with Nehemiah. Remember how he wept? The first thing he did was to ask about Jerusalem, about the house of God. When he heard, he wept. Then he was so troubled that he could not help himself. He was terrified, if you read the story because the king said, "Nehemiah, what is wrong with you?" Then Nehemiah prayed to the Lord. Remember how he lifted up his heart quietly to the Lord and he told the king the truth? The result was that Nehemiah was sent on a mission. Do you see?

The whole point is this: in the question of the testimony of Jesus, it is not a question of just mentally seeing something, it is a question of coming to a real spirit of fellowship (shall we put it?) into a fellowshipping with the Lord Jesus in His travail over the church. The testimony of Jesus has never been born easily. I look in churches today and I remember noting that the testimony of Jesus is not born easily. It has always involved terrible suffering and travail.

Here we have a man, Nehemiah, and he was not afraid to cry. He was not afraid to break down. His heart was so exercised, so deeply concerned over this whole question of the purpose of God that he was drawn into it. Very interesting. You remember how he went in the dead of the night. He told no one and he went all around the wall and he reviewed every section of the wall. Now isn't that a wonderful teacher?

What does it teach us? It teaches us that there have to be two sides. On the one side there has to be a deep, deep travail. On the other side there has to be a shattering discernment, discernment that is penetrating and piercing. Oh, this stupid sentimentality. It is pure rubbish, so that you can't *see* the thing you want to see because of this idea of love. Love speaks truth. The Scripture always says, "Love in truth." To discern. Love is not just feelings. It isn't just movie theatre love.

Behind it there's got to be a travail. There has got to be clearness. There has got to be something that is absolutely clear and yielded to the Lord. Suffering for the sake of the Lord, in the interest of Him. Those are the people who have submitted to the Lord. What a balance the Scripture always sets in these things. Before we are allowed to see what is wrong, there must be a spirit of absolute agony. Well, that's the first thing we saw.

Fellowship, Harmony and Relatedness of Function

The second thing we saw is that wonderful fellowship, the relatedness of function and harmony there has got to be if the testimony is going to be recovered. Do you remember all the goldsmiths, the perfumers, the noble ladies, the artisans, the craftsmen, and the peasants. There they all were, the lot of them. They were all apportioned to different parts of the wall. Everyone beside everyone else, each one there and they were all given a part of the wall. Every single one of them was as important as another. Noble ladies were as important, no doubt, as the peasants. Their portion on the wall was as important as any other part. If you built a beautiful wall and had one section unbuilt, the whole thing would be undone. It would be the weakness, the point of all the attack. The whole wall was important.

Well, it is a very, very wonderful record if you read it carefully and there are some very, very searching things in it. At some point, Nehemiah goes through this list of people that have done the work and I would like to know because I don't fully understand yet whether it is a criticism or a commendation? What does it mean when it says, "and so-and-so repaired the section over against his house?" What does it mean when he says, "and so-and-so repaired the section opposite his house"? I would like to know. What does it mean, when, on the other hand it says, "and so-and-so repaired another section?" I am not saying I understand. I am saying I would like to know a little bit more. What does it mean? First, when I read it, I thought it was a criticism. These people, they did not mind repairing the walls as long as it was opposite their house, or next to their house, adjoining their house. There were others who got through their part quickly. In another place it says, rather scathingly, "but their nobles put not their necks to the work." The whole point is this: they have got fellowship, a harmony, a relatedness. Everyone was appointed to a section.

Not only a fellowship of relatedness and function is necessary, but there has to be a vigilance to watch over it. That is why at one point they held their weapon in one hand and the trowel in the other. At one point when there was a breach in the wall, and they heard that the enemy was going to attack by that breach and one or two other breaches, then Nehemiah had to station a guard. Then you have men with trumpets around the wall. "If you hear the trumpet blow then all of you get to that spot." They were all together finding fellowship and harmony—each in their own place; each in their own function, all interwoven with the others.

Well, we will leave that, but you see that it is all a question of the recovery of the testimony. We all have to be placed accordingly and the Lord is looking to each one of us to fulfil our particular purpose. How many people come in and they don't want to function? Many people just stay and do nothing. The thing to do is to give yourself, abandoned, to the Lord! Abandoned, we will find it. But if you hold back till you know your function, you will never come in. If you will abandon yourself to that which is entrusted to you, you will find your function.

The Great Conflict

Then lastly, oh, the great conflict and the trial over the recovery of the testimony. This testimony is going to be bitterly contested from every side. Everything possible is going to try to get you to stop the work. There are eight definite times of opposition in this book of Nehemiah, but it never stopped the work. They are not all recorded in one chapter. They are scattered from chapter two to the end of chapter six. Oh, the opposition! (I think it was Luther who said that these eight kinds of opposition have been reproduced in every generation.)

Why didn't the opposition stop the work? It was because of the kind of character that God had produced by the Holy Spirit in the leaders. Not one of them would take it on alone; not one of them would act alone. Everyone stood like one man together in the Lord. They refused to take it on and were not moved at all. They refused at any point to come down from the building on the wall and the result was that the walls were completed.

However, the opposition did not end with the completion of the wall. That was not the end; the devil did not give up. The enemy sought to rally the forces of disaffection and faction. As soon as the walls were completed, the nobles began writing letters to Tobiah, who had led much of the troubles. Gradually, a kind of underground alliance formed which was to become a great thorn in the side of Nehemiah. As we shall find, it was thoroughly dealt with, and we shall take that up next time.

6.
Third Stage of the Return & the Testimony of Jesus

We are now dealing with the third stage of the return from the exile, the stage led by Nehemiah. You will remember that in this third stage we are dealing with something fuller than in the two previous stages. In the first stage everything was to do with the house of God and the recovery of truth in practice. The second stage is all to do with spiritual character and the third stage is all to do with rebuilding the walls of Jerusalem. However, we have found in the third stage that there has been a remarkable combination of the first two stages. All the characteristics that we found in the first two stages are now, as it were, brought together, welded together in the last stage.

You will remember that we found in the last stage, that these walls are all the more remarkable because Jerusalem was not yet built. They were building walls around, really, just the Temple and a few houses, if those were permanent. We have found that these walls symbolise the testimony of Jesus. You will remember that last time we asked ourselves a question and dwelt upon the answer: "What is the testimony of Jesus?" We speak so much about the testimony of Jesus; what really is the testimony of Jesus?

Remember we said that the testimony of Jesus, as the Holy Spirit typifies it here, is simply the welding together of two distinct things. First, is the house of God and that always comes first. The Holy Spirit has put that first and the second thing is spiritual character.

Now, you can have spiritual character outside of the house of God. You can have spiritual character in any place, and spiritual character or godliness is great gain anywhere. It is great gain for the people concerned, but not great gain to God. God does not need our godliness. God is not in need of our righteousness. God is quite sovereign and quite sufficient in that way. He does not *need* us in that sense at all. Therefore, if we are godly and righteous anywhere, that is great gain to ourselves. We shall never lose it. In the end it will certainly be judged and rewarded as such. However, godliness on certain ground is great gain to God because it is providing Him with the object of His eternal yearning. When God gets godliness on certain ground it provides Him with the material for His eternal home. The testimony of Jesus is not a personal thing, and it is not an individual thing. It is not a question of ministry, nor is it a question of groups of Christians anywhere. The testimony of Jesus is entrusted when the Lord has a people on certain clearly defined ground and when He is producing a certain spiritual character in them. When those two things are brought together and welded together you have the testimony of Jesus.

You must note the order. The walls enclosed a temple. The temple is the dwelling place of God. The walls enclosed a city and the city is the heart of a nation. So you have these two distinct things in the first and the second stage kept apart. Clearly and distinctively set out in two clear-cut stages, they are now brought together in the end. That is the testimony of Jesus.

You will remember that last time we reviewed what we had done before. We looked at the first three things to do with the recovery of the testimony of Jesus. It is possible therefore, to be on church ground and to have some building of the church without necessarily the testimony being entrusted there. The candlestick of pure gold is in the midst of those children of God gathered into Christ on the ground of their locality. This we find in the beginning of the book of Revelation. When you have that ground and you have a spiritual character, which the Lord is continually judging, you have the candlestick in its place. But it can still be there on that ground and the spiritual character can go away and the candlestick can be removed. (That is another problem that we cannot deal with now.)

Travail and Discernment

We noticed three things about the recovery of the testimony of Jesus. The first was that holding the testimony of Jesus is a matter of very real travail and of very personal, penetrating discernment. On the one side is a suffering that knocks us about so we cannot be arrogant and presumptuous or superior. On the other side is penetratingly keen, razor-edged discernment that gets right through this sentimental fluff that people call love, which isn't really love at all, but gets right down to the root of the matter and defines clearly what is wrong. You can never get to the root of any trouble until your diagnosis is absolutely hitting the point. When you have got a correct diagnosis you can do something. Otherwise, you are prodding around and messing around. Many Christians, because they are frightened of diagnosing a situation clearly and discerningly, are prodding around—activity wasted, energy wasted, service wasted, lives wasted because they are prodding around, because they are afraid. On the one side there must be a travail, on the other side there must be a razor-edged discernment that gets right to the root of the problem and is not afraid to stand alone if necessary on this question of what to touch and what not to touch.

Nehemiah got right down to the ruins. He saw the ruins, he looked into the ruins, he wept over the ruins, and he mourned over the ruins. He had a broken heart, but he saw the ruins and he was not afraid to clearly define the ruins and the rubbish that has got to be removed. In the recovery of the testimony, you cannot be held up by anything that is sheer and mere sentiment. You have got to know the ruin and you have got to see the rubbish. You have got to be able to remove the stuff that has got to be removed and you have got to be able to get down to what is the real foundation and build with the proper material. That is the first thing.

Harmony

The second thing was that there was a great harmony in the recovery of the testimony. There were all these people—aristocratic ladies, peasant ladies, perfumers, goldsmiths, silver-smiths and the rest. There were all the different people, all different classes, different types, different backgrounds, but they were all brought together and each given a place and a vigilance was needed over their fellowship together. That was the second thing and we will not spend any time on that.

Conflict and Trial

The third thing we noted was that there was great conflict and trial in this question of the recovery of the testimony. It is going to be bitterly contested. From every side, from every angle things will be said, things will be done, mud will be slung. Everything possible will be done to try to get you talking. Trying to get you to take your guard down, trying to get you to stop the work and all get turned in as you clear up the mess.

In all, there are eight definite times of opposition recorded in this book of Nehemiah, but it never stopped the work. Why did it not stop the work? It is because of the kind of character that God had produced by the Holy Spirit in the leaders. That is why. Not one of them would take it on. Not one of them would move alone. Everyone stood like a man together in the Lord. The result was that the opposition could write letters—four times—send messengers with personal letters, send prophets to give a word of the Lord to them, that all sounded so very good and all the rest of it. It did not move them at all. They refused to take it on. Sometimes they answered, but with the least words that were possible, with all good courtesy and love. Nevertheless, with absolute firmness, with absolute clarity, they refused at any point to come down from the building on the wall. The result was that the walls were completed.

As we shall find out this time, the opposition did not end with the completion of the wall. The enemy sought immediately to ally the forces of disaffection and faction. As soon as the walls were completed that was not the end. The devil did not give up. Many of the nobles (and we shall find out that the high priest was one of them) started writing letters to Tobiah, who had led much of the trouble. Gradually, a kind of alliance formed underground, which was to become a great thorn in the side of Nehemiah. As we shall find in the last chapter of this book, it was thoroughly dealt with at the last.

Lack of Self-Interest

Now, we come to another point. We have seen that the walls have been completed. Nothing could stop the completion of those walls. The conflict raged over them, but it did not stop the completion of the walls. The reason was that in the people who were building, there was a meekness and a dependence upon the Lord and a fellowship together and an utter lack of self-interest. It is an interesting thing that in Nehemiah 7:4 you will find that although the walls were completed, they set guards around. Very few people were living in Jerusalem and it says actually there were no houses built. (We know from the previous record that there were some houses, but we take it therefore that they must have been not very permanent homes. People had marked up the plots perhaps that they wished to have.) But it revealed a lack of self-interest. They were prepared, many of them, to build those walls without any real self-interest. That was the root, the heart of the Lord being able, as it were, to carry them through all these battles.

You can always be certain, that when any backsliding starts in any of our hearts, we would like to blame it on others. In actual ways, as it were, we find some reason for it elsewhere. Furthermore, we can always legitimately somehow attach some blame to others and find a reason outside of ourselves. Nevertheless, no one has ever backslidden without there being some ground inside. That is why the Lord Jesus was able to say: "the prince of this world cometh, but he has nothing in *Me*!" Let him come. He has got no foothold in the Lord. But of course, that is often not so with us. We have given ground to the enemy and he has got a foothold. Self-interest is so often this foothold Satan plays upon until at last he gets a hold.

Now we come to Nehemiah chapter seven, verse five, to the end of the chapter. Here we find a very remarkable thing. This is the exact same register as we find in Ezra chapter two. There is not a word different, so that in this one book, we have two chapters taken up with duplication. It is a most remarkable fact. For those of you who know anything about the way the Holy Spirit has compiled the Word of God, you will know quite clearly, that when the Holy Spirit duplicates something He does it for a reason. Nothing is ever duplicated in the Word of God without a reason. Now, why have we got the exact same register, taking up approximately seventy verses, twice repeated, within a few chapters of each other? In Ezra chapter two and in Nehemiah chapter seven, it is the same register given twice. In fact, Nehemiah refers back to it. In verse five it tells you that he refers right back to that genealogy of those that came out with Zerubbabel. He clearly tells us what register he is looking at.

Pure Pedigree

What do we learn from this? The fourth thing that we learn about the recovery of the testimony is this: the necessity of continual vigilance over, and I want you to note the vital importance of history and pedigree. That is a funny thing to say, but note the vital importance of history and pedigree. If you look at Ezra 2:59–63, you will find that some of them could not prove their pedigree. I am afraid Zerubbabel and Joshua (Jeshua) were very hard on them. They put them out of the priesthood. They were allowed to stay in the land, but they were put out of the priesthood until a high priest could stand up with the Urim and the Thummim and would be able to distinguish whether they really had a pedigree. in the holding of the testimony of Jesus. I will repeat that again. The fourth thing that we learn about the recovery of the testimony of Jesus is the necessity of continual vigilance over, and pure pedigree in the holding of the testimony of Jesus.

Now, why does the Holy Spirit emphasise this so strongly by giving this register twice? Will you note the two times that it comes? The first time this register appears it is to do with the building of the house of God. The second time this register appears it is to do with the recovery of the testimony of Jesus. Mark carefully that no attention is drawn to any register in the second stage. Only in the first and the third stage is our attention drawn to this very important register, by which everyone could determine their pedigree and therefore determine their right to responsibility. Let us make it absolutely clear right away now. This did not determine their right to a portion of the land. It determined their right to responsibility.

That is where we are going to learn our fourth great lesson in this book of Ezra/Nehemiah. You see, we have found that the Holy Spirit obviously feels that this matter of pedigree, as we call it, spiritual pedigree, is of vital, paramount importance when it comes to the question of responsibility. Why does the Holy Spirit give no genealogy, although there must have been such registry, why does He not draw our attention to a register in the second stage? It is because, the second stage is to do with spiritual character. You can have spiritual character in exile. You can have spiritual character in Persia. You can have spiritual character in Babylon. You can have spiritual character anywhere in the Dispersion. You can have it anywhere. You do not need a register for that. That is spiritual life. God, because He is Father of His people, because He is the Father of His family, has given us life, and will develop that life as much as He can. You find that out in the book of Esther. There is no mention of the things of God, no mention of the house of God, no mention of the land of God, no mention even of God's name, and yet, spiritual character. Do you see? There was no need of a register. What does Esther need a register for? She was queen! What did Mordecai need a register for? He did not need a register. You only need a register when you have got back to the land.

However, when it came to participating in the building of the house of God, or when it came to participating in the building of the walls of Jerusalem, you needed a register. You needed to prove your pedigree. That is very important. If there was one area where we as a company started off on a weak footing, it was in this question of responsibility. I will speak about that in a moment. We had been confused at the beginning over this whole question of responsibility. We started off on the wrong foot and it is only now that we are beginning to see that we have got to get onto the other foot in the right way.

The Register

Now, what does this chapter really teach us? Or shall I put it this way: what do these two chapters, Ezra two and Nehemiah seven, really teach us? They teach us simply this (let me just tell you exactly what it means): before Nehemiah, the governor, repopulated or even before he would consider repopulating Jerusalem with inhabitants, he insisted on having a register to ensure pure blood. He insisted. Jerusalem stands, as we have already said, for the testimony of Jesus. That is the first thing. The second thing was this: before they would settle the question of the courses of the priests and the courses of the Levites in the house of God, Nehemiah insisted on having that register out and making sure that every priest and every Levite operating in the house of God had a clear, pure, pedigree behind him. So when it comes to living in Jerusalem, or when it comes to working within the house of God, Nehemiah insists on a pedigree. He insists on it.

If you will look at Nehemiah 7:61–65 you will find a rather shocking thing. (I believe we drew attention to it in Ezra 2.) Here there are some good and seemingly faithful people who could not prove their pedigree and they were put out. On the one hand, they were not allowed to live within Jerusalem, and on the other hand, they were put out of the priesthood. Now, just sit back and think for a moment. Think what it would mean. These men have come all the way back from exile. These people believed that they were utterly faithful. They had come and had left everyone else in the exile and now how were they rewarded? When they get back to the land, they find that man called Ezra and a man called Nehemiah get up and say, "We are very, very sorry. You cannot prove your pedigree. You're out. We are very sorry about it. Very sorry. You can live with us. You can participate in the good of the land. You can participate in the services of our God, but you cannot have any responsibility given to you or entrusted to you whatsoever." Well, isn't that a severe thing when you really think about it? It is a severe thing. It is a terrible thing. After all these people came back, was it their fault that somehow or other they were lost?

Now, why does the Holy Spirit take hold of this so severely and handle these people so seemingly harshly? It is because He is teaching us a tremendous lesson. They may have been perfectly good men. They may have served well in exile—and this is the hardness of it—they could still serve well if they went back to the exile. If those people had said, "All right then, if you do not want us here we will pack our bags and go home. We will go back. We will go back to Babylon." They could have gone back to Babylon and you know they would have been welcomed in the first synagogue. They could have operated and functioned as priests and Levites in the exile. But Nehemiah would not let them function and operate as priests and Levites in Jerusalem, or in the house of

God, or in the land. Why are these two things totally different? Why should the priests be allowed to operate there in exile if they are not allowed to operate in the land? Do you see now what we are getting at? There are two clearly defined realms, that Esther will teach us very clearly, two clearly defined realms. It seemingly means that God deals with us in one realm altogether differently than the way He deals with us in the other. He will allow certain things, He will bless certain things, He will use certain things in one realm, but He will not do it in the other. We come right up against a veto. We can fight it. We can press about it. It can cause us great irritation, but we know we are up against a veto in the other realm. We cannot behave as we did in that realm, in this realm. Do you see? We cannot just, as it were, do here what we did there. We come up against a divine veto. The Holy Spirit immediately says, "No." It is a question of pedigree. We do not talk about pedigree in that realm, but here it is a question of pedigree. We want to know your pedigree.

The Necessity of Clarity

We have to see that very, very clearly for this reason: we have to see that in recovery, at each stage of it there is a necessity of pure, clear, uncontaminated history. Can I put it another way? It is not so much a question of actual mixture, as a question of clarity. Have you got that understood? Those men may not have had a taint of foreign blood in their history. They may have been as pure as Nehemiah himself, but they could not prove it! And because they could not prove it, they were not clear. They were deemed unclean. What does it mean? It means they were not clear.

Not clear. So they could not be used. They could not be brought in. They could not be given responsibility. They had to stay out. Do you understand that? Those men may have been good men, they may have been moral men, and they may have been upright men. They may have been a good sight better than many of the others, but they were put out.

Now what does that really, basically teach us? It teaches us this: If they are not clear, or we are not clear about their pedigree then there can be no responsibility given to them whatsoever. They may be obviously partners with us in common life. They may be obviously one with us in the Lord Jesus. The distinction is not made between life; it is made over responsibility. This is the point that we have to understand so utterly clearly if we are going to understand principles of the last days.

As we have said, Ezra and Nehemiah contain principles of the last days. Just in the same way that I and II Timothy and Titus contain principles for the last days. What are these principles? Here is one of these principles: we are absolutely one with all the people of God. We are absolutely one in an even more obvious and outward way with anyone who will come onto what we call 'church ground.' However, just because we are all found on church ground does not mean that responsibility can be given to anyone. We have got to be absolutely clear as to a person's pedigree. This is where we started off on the wrong step. We have made a mixture and a confusion on the one side of our tremendous emphasis upon one life, not truth, but life. "Life is the thing; we must stress life. We are one because of the life, absolutely one." That is absolutely so. But that does not mean for one single moment, that therefore we can give responsibility to anyone, anybody. It could mean quite the opposite.

How then should we determine this question of responsibility? It is a question of clarity. That is all. You see, they wanted to be absolutely sure that there was no Egyptian influence. No Edomite influence. No Moabite influence. No Canaanite influence. No Babylonian, no Persian influence. They wanted to be absolutely sure that people taking responsibility were absolutely 100% clear. If they were, the whole thing was open and responsibility given. Otherwise, they must wait until a priest rose up with Urim and the Thummim, who could determine once and for all whether they were really clear or not. It was the whole question of responsibility.

Our dear brother Lee said to us and this shocked so many, "We are one. We accept everyone at the Lord's Table. We will refuse no one who is a believer at the Lord's Table. That is our testimony to our one life in Christ; but we reserve the right in administration and in ministry to narrow it down to those that we know are clear. This is an end time principle." You can't have any Tom, Dick, and Harry just coming in in these days and just hand everything over as people think we should. You cannot just throw in your lot with anyone. There are these two clear realms. We are one. It may not seem it, but we are one. However, we are one on certain ground.

"We are absolutely one," as they could have said in those days, "with those who are in exile, but we will not touch them. We will not go back to them. They come back to us; we will not go back to them. We are one." When all of the offerings were offered in the house of God, what were they for? They were for the twelve tribes of Israel, although very few would ever return they were for the lot. It was always for everyone, for all. It was inclusive, never exclusive.

For all those that had come back to the land, it was more practical than that, much more practical. They were there to participate in the privileges of being actually on the land, within the land. They were in living touch with the testimony. They were in living touch with the house of God. But as far as responsibility went, no one living on that ground could be given it unless they were clear.

Do you see the complete difference between that and the beginning? In David's day, in Solomon's day there was no talk about this. No one talked about genealogies, making them clear. No one talked about it. In the New Testament, at the beginning of the church, there was no talk about it. Now here we come to a very, very important point. There was no talk in the beginning of the New Testament, at the beginning of the church, of this question, as far as it was concerned, it was free. We were all, not only one in the Lord Jesus, but were clear. Since those days a tremendous amount has happened. The whole thing has gone into exile. The whole thing has fallen away. The whole thing has become a terrible mixture of Babylon and Egypt, so that now it is woven into the very fabric of those that are the Lord's, into their very being, into their very context, the very atmosphere, the whole thing has seeped into it.

Paul's Letters to Timothy

Now why did Paul write I Timothy and II Timothy? Have you ever thought? He expressly tells us that it is for the end times when there shall be a great falling away. What does he say? "No man can be an elder, unless ..." Unless, unless, unless, unless! "No man can be a deacon, unless ..." Unless, unless, unless! What is he doing? Is he giving, as many think, qualifications? No, he is saying simply this one thing: We have got to be clear on pure pedigree. Do you know how he says it? He says that in a great house there are vessels to honour and vessels to dishonour. "Let a man purge himself," he says, of those vessels of dishonour. What a thing to say of the Lord's people, but that is what it says. Purge himself of vessels of dishonour. They are around, but let him stand pure and clear before the Lord with a pure, clear pedigree before God. He said, "The foundation of God standeth sure." Isn't that wonderful? "The foundation of God standeth sure. And let him that nameth the name of the Lord depart from iniquity."

Do you see? Those letters are all to do with the kind of pedigree we have got to look for. What kind of family has he got? What is his wife like? What are his children like? How does he behave himself at work? Do you see that all these point to his pedigree? Where does he stand in the house of God? What does Paul say? "I have written these things that a man might know how he ought to behave himself in the house of the living God." Do you see? It is a question of responsibility. It is a question of responsibility, not a question of life. Paul never said, "divide from them." Paul never said, "leave them." If they are on church ground you cannot leave them. You have got to stay with them. But he said: Don't you become contaminated. That pedigree has got to be kept for the Lord.

Well, there is a tremendous amount there, which, no doubt, raised a lot of questions. But you will see, straightaway, that it is not a question of the general lack of the nation. It is not a question of its general life. All who are on this ground are participants in the general life. It is a question of responsibility. It is not a question of life; it is a question of responsibility. The distinction is made, not over life, but over responsibility. This is what we have got to come to: in the end we have got to be absolutely clear on this question of responsibility. We as a people have got to come to it. We have got to have courage—and it takes courage—literal courage, to be able to stand on this way. It takes a man like Nehemiah and a people like that to have that courage. You see how they, as it were, handled this kind of situation.

The Word of God and Our History

Well, there we are, that one great point, and what is the last great point? (Well, actually there are two more, but the very last one is a small one.) What is the last big point that we learn in the question of the third stage of the recovery? It is from chapter eight and goes right through chapters 8—12. It is a very big portion. Now what is it? What is the lesson we learn? Well, I have put it like this. In the recovery we must have a further instruction in, an understanding of, and a complete committal to the Word of God and our history. Now, I want you to take very careful note of this. I will say it again. In recovery we must have a thorough instruction in, an understanding of, and a complete committal to the Word of God and our history.

Now, let's look at these chapters. Nehemiah 8:1: "The first day of the seventh month …", the great conference. It was one month after the walls had been completed. One month had now elapsed. The genealogies, the register, had been taken out; things had been sorted out. Evidently, it was a little more clear. Now a big conference was called, a period of a big conference. This big conference lasted in a rather scattered way over at least a month. All the people of God came from the far north and the far south; they journeyed up to Jerusalem for this great conference. It was a tremendous affair if you look at it.

The first thing you find is this: and it is really rather lovely the way the writer has put it: "And they read in the book, the law of God, distinctly; and they gave the sense." (That is not always so.) But the law was read distinctly and the sense was given. You see in Nehemiah 8:8: "They read in the book, the law of God distinctly; and they gave the sense, so that they understood the reading." Isn't that wonderful? The other word is a technical word, by the way, used in the Persian Empire for reading an official document in Aramaic and it being translated at the same time into the vernacular of the people concerned. So it may well be that there were some who just did not understand Hebrew, and as it was read in Hebrew, distinctly and clearly, so it was also interpreted for those that did not understand and the Levites went throughout the whole crowd making absolutely sure that everyone understood. Anyone who did not understand put their hand up or something like that. And the Levite came and said, "Well, this is what it means." This is exactly what that means. Now isn't that wonderful?

Never in the history of the people of God had such a conference ever taken place. For the most part it was a little handful that understood and the rest were left in ignorance. They just enjoyed the family, you know, like a fellowship sort-of thing. But this time it was absolutely brought down to each one so that they have got the understanding.

Now the first day of the month the Law was read to everyone. Ezra spent most of the day reading. Then it says, if you look carefully in verse 13 and following, then they had all the leaders together—the priests, the Levites, and the rulers of the fathers' houses. They all came together, for, shall we put it this way, a great inner conference of responsible leadership. Here is the interesting point if you read that entire following paragraph. What happened? Ezra, and the scribes, the Levites, they teach those leaders deeply, deeply on the whole question of the Word of God and their history and what is the immediate result? All the leaders say, "Well! Do you know what we should be doing now? It is the seventh month. We should have the feast of Tabernacles and we are not keeping it. Let's look. They started to look and they found it exactly. Since the days of Joshua the son of Nun there had never been a Feast of Tabernacles kept quite like that. They told everyone! They said, "We have understood the Word. We have really understood the Word and our history.

Do you see what was beginning to happen? Ezra had it on his heart, as William Tyndale did, to see that the poorest and most ignorant person understood the Word of God and understood their history. So, he got the leaders together and he instructed them. Then they had a seven-day festival and the next day, a solemn assembly lasting the whole of the eighth day. Every single day they read the Law. Every day the same method, as it were, was kept. So that you see, for the first time in the history of the people of God, a new sense of the meaning of the Law of the Word of God and their history dawned upon them.

On the twenty-fourth day of the month it reached its climax, a whole day given. Everyone gathered together. If you read carefully, it is rather lovely. There was a small wooden platform, up which Ezra went, that was specially built with certain steps; quite a new innovation. Evidently, they had never had such a thing. It clearly says that Ezra was in the sight of all the people— quite the new innovation evidently—and read quite clearly to them all. Then on the twenty-fourth day, what did they do? They spent the whole day. The first quarter of the daylight hours they spent in reading the Word of God. The last half of the day they spent in confession and worship. Three hours of one, three hours of the other. What a tremendous thing it all really is! It was the climax. And the whole people waited on God in contrition and repentance, humbly, in the light of His Word and their history. There had never been a day like it. It says the people wept.

Do you know what Ezra had to do? He had to tell everyone, "Don't tell them not to weep!" The first day, he told them not to weep. They must all give presents to everyone else and everyone must be happy and joyful. But on the twenty-fourth day of course, they all did weep. That was the day when they put earth on their heads. They wore sackcloth and dust and ashes and they waited. What did they wait for? They waited on God that they might truly and clearly understand His Word and their history. Never had there been such a day. Never had the whole people wept. Oh yes, leaders had wept over the people. But never had the people wept because they understood the Law of God and realised that they had broken it. They understood their history for the first time and realised what fools they had been! Why did it all come about?

Do you understand what was happening? In this recovery the people were grasping the whole idea behind it. Do you understand? They were, as it were, understanding God's Word for the first time and the whole thing was just opening up before them as a vast panorama. They were beginning to understand God's Word and they were beginning to understand their own tragic history. Do you see? What a tremendous thing it all really was!

They were all so instructed that they understood their recent history in the light of their past history. Now that is a very, very important thing. They were so instructed in the Word of God that they understood the exile. You see we haven't got it all. We have only got a little tiny portion and as always in the Word we have been given much more of the beginning. I do not know whether it is human or whether I ought to say it, but so often, it seems to me that the person who is writing it all down seems to have become so tired at the end that they just stop. Often in these great speeches, you find a tremendous amount at the beginning and then it tails off to just a little sort-of framework at the end. You will find that here. It gets right down to King David and then we just get a very, very quick tracing. But the important thing to see is this: they understood the exile and they understood their return, in the light of their past history. They went back to the beginning. They went back to Abraham. They went back to Moses. They went back to the Exodus. They understood the golden calf. They understood the entry into the land. They understood the period of the judges. They were so adamant. "We understand! We understand our history. For the first time we understand!" Do you see it?

Understanding God's Word and God's Purpose

Then in chapter nine we find a great covenant made. It is a wonderful covenant. I love the covenant that they made because they were so thorough. They went through statutes and ordinances. They committed themselves to the Law of God. They reviewed the whole covenant. They went right through the tithes, the ordinances—everything, you see? Now, what do we learn here? We learn this: in every movement of the Holy Spirit for recovery, it is essential that we understand God's Word—we understand God's Word—and that we understand His eternal purpose as a governing factor in everything. We understand it. Every one of us, if we are by the grace of God in such a movement of the Spirit, we should to be able to say what is the purpose of God. We should be able to have some understanding of the Word of God. We should have an understanding of our time. We should be able to understand God's dealings with His people so that we understand His dealings with us. We should so understand God's Word, we should so understand God's purpose, we should so understand God's dealings with His people through the ages that we understand how we, in our age and generation, are related to it. We are only a continuation. We should understand. Do you see?

This is the tragedy of today. There are hundreds of Christians, many dear, beloved brothers and sisters who have really studied the Bible and yet when you speak with them, they have hardly any real idea what the thing's about! They know a verse here and they could preach a message on a verse there. They know there is a verse in the back and they could preach a message on that verse. But if you say, "What is the meaning of Abraham?"

They would just look at you, "Oh, it is faith." Is that all Abraham means? Faith? What is the meaning of Abraham? What is the meaning of the Exodus? What is the meaning of the Tabernacle? What is the meaning of the Temple? What is the meaning of the monarchy? What is the meaning of these things? We should know!

If someone says to you, "What is the Church?" You ought to understand what the Church is. You ought to be able to say what the Church is. What is God's eternal purpose? You ought to be able to say what is God's eternal purpose. You may not be able to write some great theological treatise on it, but you ought to be able, almost intuitively, to put your finger upon the thing. Do you see what I mean?

In other words, we should have an intelligent, a spiritually intelligent, understanding of God's Word. It should not be as a kind of textbook for preaching and not as a kind of a collection of texts for gospel messages. Nor should it be as a kind of book from which we can get systems of doctrines and systems of truth. We ought to know the Word of God as God's letter to us, God's revelation to us. We ought to handle it with reverence. Be careful how we speak. We ought to know what is the theme. Why is there a tree of life? Can you tell me what the meaning of the tree of life is? Why is there a tree of life at the beginning and a tree of life at the end? Why is there a garden at the beginning and a city at the end? See? We should know these things. What is the meaning of them?

God has given us His Word and everything depends upon His Word. In every movement of recovery it is absolutely essential that we understand the Word of God, not in bits and pieces, and not just for a devotional. Now, don't get me wrong. Obviously, the Word of God is there for our encouragement, and help, and comfort, and consolation. However, it is not just like *The Daily Light*; you know a little thing you turn out for help each day to guide you. It is not just that. Many people absolutely prostitute the Bible—that is the only word—they prostitute it by using it as a kind of funny little textbook. And at the end what have they got? They do not know. They know it personally in the sense that they could say, "'Cast thy bread upon the waters; and after many days it shall come back to me.' Oh, that helped me in such and such a year." That is wonderful; that is personal experience, but could you please tell me what lies behind all of that. Do you see? We ought to *understand* the Word of God in an intelligent way. The Bible has not just been given to us so we can get a few little tips now and again when we are in trouble. It has been given to us that we might have a spiritually intelligent understanding of our calling and vocation; that we understand where we are going and where we have come from, and how we are getting there. That is what the Bible is for; it is for our instruction.

The Work of the Holy Spirit

Now, if we are going to be in any way brought into such a move of the Holy Spirit, we are going to find that one of the most elementary things is that the Holy Spirit is not going to let any of us get away. He is going to bring down all these things to us and those of us who are responsible have got to see that, as far as it lies within us, the Word of God is given distinctly. The sense is put into it so people are able to understand. Do you see?

How important that all is! Really, as you know, we can save an awful lot of trouble if people understood the Word of God. Oh! Things sometimes that Christians come out with—I almost wish they kept their mouths shut and hid their ignorance. But you know how something suddenly comes out and we just say something. The Word of God would turn it upside down in an instant if they knew it. There is something there in every single situation which can be interpreted by all that God is doing. So we just ought to understand that.

We ought also to understand Church history. Very few Christians have any understanding of Church history. Therefore they do not understand what God is doing in our generation because they have not understood Church history. We ought to understand Church history, not as something dry because it is not dry! It is very thrilling once you really get down to it. If you really start to study Church history and if you will begin to put yourself under the Holy Spirit's headship, if you put yourself under the anointing you will begin to understand where we come in. You will begin to discern an amazing pattern in Church history, which is absolutely typified in Chronicles and Ezra and Nehemiah. You will find it. There is no mistake about it. It is there. It traces it right through. You will find it.

You see, there is an amazing battle on over these centuries for the recovery of something which has been terribly lost. The battle is on—bit by bit, part by part—something has been recovered, something has been uncovered, something has been established only once again to, as it were, die down. But you see the whole point is that the Holy Spirit is in charge of this operation.

It is what the Lord said to Zerubbabel by the prophet: "Not by might, nor by power, but by My Spirit, saith the Lord of hosts. Who art thou, O great mountain? before Zerubbabel thou shalt become a plain and he shall bring forth the top stone with shoutings of Grace, grace unto it." Do you understand? The Holy Spirit is in charge. It is not by might, nor by power, nor any other thing; the Holy Spirit is doing something. If we look through Church history, we shall understand our own recent history in the light of past history. We shall understand it in the light of God's Word. Do you see how important this is?

I also want you to note the immediate response that there was in the people's hearts to God's Word. They covenanted to give themselves immediately; they yielded themselves up to it and the names of every single person who wrote their signature under the covenant is there. Do you see all that they covenant to? They covenant themselves under a curse and an oath. What a terrible thing! In other words, if they break this covenant the curse is on them. What an abandonment to the Word of God! What an abandonment to their history! You see? They understood. How they spoke of Him as the great and terrible God, but great in love and faithful in compassion. (See Nehemiah 9:32.) They understood it all.

Isn't it wonderful that right back there, literally, a millennium or two ago, a man called Ezra understood the change in Abram's name? In his prayer he was able to say, "Abram, whom Thou gavest the name of Abraham." He understood Church history, Old Testament Church history. He understood it. He got the thing clear! I am quite sure that if I asked many people out there: Can you tell me why the Lord changed Abram to Abraham?

Everyone would be blank. There is tremendous significance in every point in the Word of God. You see? He had got it! He got hold of the thing and responded and gave himself to it. Oh, everything else started to come out then. They committed themselves to God's Law, to His Word, to His statutes, to His ordinances, to His festivals, to the jubilee year. They had not kept the jubilee year ... where anyone who is in debt to us, we will let them go free. Slaves amongst us, they may all pack off home. They can go. They covenanted; that means a lot. See, it is coming down to practical points now, isn't it? It is all very well to rejoice and weep over the Word. But, oh my word, if you have got a big house and you have been brought up with lots of slaves and two years hence is Jubilee, you have got to say goodbye to half of them. Then you might begin to realise how very difficult it was. You see?

We could say all other kinds of things, too. It came down to practice. Then they said: tithes. "Oh Lord, the tithe. We will give Thee the tithe; all of the tithe we will give." Then they said the first fruits—yes they offered the first fruits—everything. Everything! They went through the whole list of all the first fruits they were going to give to the Lord—the wine, the grain, the oil, right down to the sheep and everything else. They were going to give the first fruits to the Lord.

But do you see what had happened? They covenanted. They understood their history. It says now that they understand it. The house of God is the heart. The city is the hub of it. We understand. We will promise. We will enter into a covenant with the Lord that we will never forsake the House of God. We will never forsake the House of God. We will always owe our allegiance to this spot.

Then you know a very wonderful thing follows straight on, a thing that most people overlook. In the first verse of chapter eleven it says that they cast lots. One man in ten was to live in Jerusalem. Do you know what that means? Think about it. They cast lots amongst all the people. One man in ten is a tenth of the nation. Now what does that mean? Well think! It means that Jerusalem is a tithe. Jerusalem is a first fruit! One in ten. They had promised to give all the other tithes to the Lord, now they said the city itself is first fruits.

Now, we have to stop there, but you will understand quite a lot of the book of Revelation if you understand it from that light. Everyone who offered willingly, freely offered himself. They blessed them. (It is rather funny I think). The others, their lot came to them, but they blessed those that willingly offered. Of all the people there, you see, not everyone wanted to live in the city. They knew that it was not quite so nice living in the city behind the walls as being out in a nice little olive orchard. Most of them wanted to live outside the city. They did not want the restriction and the limitation of the city. So they had to cast lots. It is rather a sad thing isn't it? But the point behind it all is that one-tenth and those who willingly offered were the population of the city. Of course, we understand now it is pure pedigree. That is all in the background. It is clear. But from the whole, a tenth. It was a first fruit—a tithe, a glorious tithe.

Then, what do the people see? They see that the temple and the city are the heart and the hub of everything. They see the city and the temple as the heart of their ministry and their vocation. Now that is a big point. They just see that. Their vocation as a people is bound up here.

Well, that is nearly the end of Nehemiah. Chapter twelve is just the dedication of the wall. If only we had the time to spend on the dedication, because it is rather lovely in one way. Ezra leads one company right down that side of the wall and Nehemiah leads a company right down the other. The two great leaders of the two last stages leading the companies. They sang and they sang and they sang until at last they met, just in front of the House of God on the wall. There they had a great time of worship and praise. The two companies met together. They encircled the city with praise. The words of Isaiah came true: "Thy walls Salvation, thy gates Praise" (see Isaiah 60:18b) ... and they shall sing. Do you remember how Isaiah said that they shall come back and they shall sing? That was literally fulfilled in those days. They sang on the walls, the recovered walls, and the whole population was just one great choir of praises.

It is wonderful thing really, when you think of it. This was the end. But of course, this has given me a great problem actually, Nehemiah for some strange reason does not end there! And I have been telling you the dedication of the wall is in the thirteenth chapter. But unfortunately, I have found that the dedication of the wall is not in the thirteenth chapter, it was in the twelfth chapter. The thirteenth chapter just did not seem to make sense. It was all to do with rather strange reform. The first thing was over mixed marriage. What did they suddenly discover? After all this reading of the Word, after all this study of the Word, someone suddenly discovered that somewhere in Deuteronomy it said, "No Ammonite or Moabite shall enter into the assembly of the Lord's house; even to the tenth generation" (see Dt. 23:3). "Oh! Nehemiah, we must be obedient," and they gave themselves to this. It says the whole congregation separated themselves. No foreigner was ever allowed within the priesthood of the Lord's house from that day.

But do you know what happened? I think Nehemiah must have smiled even though he had to first turn the other cheek. He suddenly discovered that his old friend Tobiah was an Ammonite and that simply meant that Tobiah was now, once and forever, excluded. He had led all the opposition and because he had married a Jewess, and his son was married, we understand, in some alliance with the high priest, the high priest had given him a room in the courts of the Lord's house. Nehemiah says (if you read it, it is all rather wonderful, it is all in the first person, it is his own account): "I went there. I took hold of Tobiah's household furniture and stuff and I threw it out! I threw it out! I cleansed the room!" In other words he looked upon it as thoroughly defiled. That was the end of Tobiah. He was out.

Then Nehemiah found that the tithes were not brought in. All the Levites had gone back because they were not being looked after. They were supposed to be living, as it were, by faith but no one looked after them, so they found that they could not live at all, so they went back to the land. Nehemiah said, "Come on, come up! You all come back. Something is wrong here." He put faithful men in the treasury and he told the people what he thought, if you read carefully, about the Lord's people covenanting. "Oh," they said, "we have covenanted, and so soon, we have broken the covenant."

Then there was the Sabbath. Well, what was happening on the Sabbath? The merchants from Tyre were bringing in their fish and fish stores, and they were coming just inside the gate on the

Sabbath. Of course, as poor Nehemiah said: If the Lord's people weren't going to buy from them, then it would all stop, but the Lord's people were going out to buy. So he said, "Shut the gates on the Sabbath." At sunset on Friday, the gates were shut. Then what did the Tyrenian traders do? They set their stores up outside the gate and people went out of the small side gates to buy.

So, if you read again you will find how Nehemiah went down, as it were, and shook his fist at these fish people and said, "Look here, if you stay here another Sabbath I will lay hands on you." They were never seen again from that day to this. They went. Do you see what happened? He took hold of these men saying, "If you come here, I will lay hands on you." You read it. I am not using slang. They were gone in a flash.

Then poor Nehemiah, he suddenly found out after all these covenants, that there were mixed marriages. To his horror he heard little children speaking half in the language of Ashdod and half in the language of God's people. It was terrible for Nehemiah. "Oh!" He thought, "All our suffering, the word of God, our history, and all the instruction and now look what they are doing!" I am afraid Nehemiah was not exactly kind. If you read, it says he pulled their hair out; he dealt with them very severely. He thoroughly pained them and punished them and he said they all grieved tremendously. But then our old friend Sanballat comes into the picture and we suddenly find there wasn't obedience. Sanballat's son, if I am right, was son-in-law to the high priest. He had married the high priest's daughter. It shows you, doesn't it, how you somehow find treachery and superficiality in high places. Well, it happened. Evidently, when everyone else agreed to separate, Sanballat's son refused. So it says another lovely little instance happened: Nehemiah chased him bodily. Oh, you see the aged Nehemiah running now, chasing him right out!

The Necessity of Watchfulness

What does that all teach us? Well, I want you to see that the last lesson is this: the necessity of watchfulness in the nature of the testimony. All of this had happened. All this had taken place. Now as soon as the people had covenanted, as soon as they were on the advent of the Messiah's appearing, it all begins to slide a bit.

Well, Nehemiah is a wonderful story, a wonderful man, and apart from that a wonderful spiritual character was produced in him. But you see on the one side no sympathy, on the other side true travail. On the one side you see that which is utterly uncompromising and thorough, on the other side that which is full of love and understanding. That is the only way we should ever get through in this question of the testimony of Jesus.

These little things, what were they really? They were the rights of the Lord, weren't they? His right to us corporately, together, nothing else. He is jealous for that. He doesn't want anything else. He wants us. No membership, you know, where it is half and half, all mixed up. He wants His people to be pure. He is jealous for that. There is no Moabite, no Ammonite, nothing else like that in the congregation of the Lord's people. When I speak of the congregation, I mean of course the Church, not the assembly.

Then there is tithing, His right to our money, and Sabbath, His right to our time. These are only just the guarantee of the rest of the law. The Sabbath and tithes are only first fruits of the rest of the law, just a guarantee, a seal, a sign, an evidence of His right to our very being.

How deceived we have been! We have a deception within. That is the tragedy! Do you know we have listened to that deception? How it lies! That is really the tragedy. If you were only to take the Word of God and look at every time there has been backsliding, you see it always begins with deception. Someone becomes deluded. They suddenly say, "Oh, this ... oh, that. The world is so nice. How happy the world seems, how carefree. I would love to be there." We have seen that. We have seen people who have gone back. They have committed suicide; that is the only way to say it. They are living corpses. It is a terrible, terrible testimony! What to? To a delusion, deception. What is the root of this thing? Mixture. Just opening the door a bit. That is what we mean by pure pedigree. That mixture must not come in.

So Ezra and Nehemiah from beginning to end are driving a wedge right the way through. Oh, they are not going to put everyone out. All they are going to do is just simply say: in this question of life, we have purity when it is a question of responsibility.

Well, that is a wonderful way to finish Nehemiah. When at the end of Old Testament history, we are now at the very advent, as far as Scripture is concerned, of the coming of the Lord Jesus. With Nehemiah the curtain comes down; that is the end. It is the finish of Old Testament history. Now we go back to Job and Psalms and all the other prophets and look at the prophecy, but the Old Testament history is at an end. We have only got Esther and Esther precedes Nehemiah. Do you see?

What are these books for, Ezra and Nehemiah? Simply but wonderfully, the Holy Spirit is out to recover something which has been terribly lost. He! He will do it in cooperation with how ever small a number come onto that right ground. Get them onto that ground and He will do it. All the characteristics that we find in Ezra and Nehemiah will be made true ... in us. It will be there. The Holy Spirit is in charge. He will recover it. It may seem to us that the purpose of God is utterly submerged in error, and ignorance, and exile. It is all right. We do not have to worry about that at all. Why is that so? Because if the Holy Spirit is on the move He can find those that will come with Him and be pliable in His hand. He will recover the purpose of God gloriously and realise it. He will bring us right out to the advent of the Lord's coming.

I do not know how long we have. We may have many years. In future years we may go down in history as some queer movement, as it were, but nevertheless something the Holy Spirit did right back there in the middle ages we may be called then. We don't know. On the other hand we may well be right in the end of the last stage of the end of the end of the end. There may be years ahead, but still the end.

So, what have we learned? We have learned that we cannot do anything in ourselves; only the Holy Spirit can do it. However, the Holy Spirit does not do it alone. He does it in us. In us! Give ourselves to the Holy Spirit and the purpose of God will be realised though all hell stands against it and we shall find ourselves at the brink of the coming of the Lord. The conditions will have been made true for His coming and He will return. May the Lord help us to understand such a lesson.

7.
An Introduction to the Book of Esther

The Holy Spirit not only set His heart on recovering all that had been lost in Chronicles, but this is how He actually recovered it. Not only how He purposed and determined to recover it, but how in actual fact, He did recover it. I want to remind you that, really, with the end of the book of Nehemiah the whole scene is set for the coming of the Messiah. The conditions are fulfilled, the people are in the land, the city is being rebuilt, the house of God is functioning, everything is now prepared. As far as sacred history goes, it is the end. As far as sacred history goes, the next thing is the Messiah. The next thing is the birth of Jesus. We have to underline that because, you see, the Holy Spirit, in a wonderful way, has now placed the book of Esther after Ezra and Nehemiah although, in one sense, it does not belong there. We have got to recognise why the Holy Spirit has taken (and you shall see that in a moment), why the Holy Spirit has placed it where He has placed it now in the Scriptures.

You will remember that even if it is only a faithful and afflicted remnant that have returned, that faithful and afflicted remnant have given God the conditions and the means which He requires to fulfil all His age-long promises and purpose concerning His Son and a people for Himself. We have learned that if God's purpose seems to be submerged beneath error and ignorance and contradiction and compromise, it is not too great a task for the Holy Spirit. The Holy Spirit only has to have a nucleus that is abandoned to Him, and all that seems so impossible melts away. All that seems to be just absolutely an impossible, insoluble, invincible barrier to the Lord getting the condition He requires for the coming of the Messiah or for getting the means that He requires for the coming of the Messiah although it may all seem so impossible and improbable, the Holy Spirit is sufficient. That really is the simple lesson of Ezra/Nehemiah.

With that we closed last time. Later on when we come to the prophets and begin to fit them in to this background that we have already built, we shall begin to understand their ministry, for instance, Zechariah's great ministry. Do you remember when he continually talked about this great mountain becoming a plain? "Not by might, nor by power, but by My Spirit," and so on, all begins to take a new meaning, it gives us a new insight into what the Lord wants to do in our own day and generation.

The wonderful thing that we can write over Ezra/Nehemiah is simply this: the last word is always God's. If you forget everything else you might remember that the last word is always God's. Sometimes when we look at the state of the church today and we know the *conditions* that the Lord wants and needs and requires for the coming again of the Lord Jesus, the *means* that He wants for the coming again of the Lord Jesus, whilst it all may seem to be so impossible, so improbable, and so insuperable; yet, with the Holy Spirit, there is not one single thing that can stand in the way.

The Literary Style

Now we come to the book of Esther. Esther is one of the only two books in the Bible that bear the name of a woman, which, in itself, makes it remarkable. The other book is the book of Ruth. I trust most of you have read Esther because you will not find it difficult. Once you set yourself to the task you will find it an exceedingly fascinating little book. It is quite dramatic. Without being irreverent, it is almost like a thriller once you get into it. You will be immediately arrested by the complete difference of atmosphere and of surroundings and of everything in the little book of Esther. I think you will be very much arrested by its vital and direct style. It does not waste words. The little book of Esther wastes no words. There is no repetition There is nothing of that kind at all. It is very direct and it is vital in its style.

You will also notice that it is a book that differs completely from almost all the other books of the Old Testament in its atmosphere. In actual fact, it is different from the books of the whole Bible, but particularly of the books of the Old Testament. I think you only have to read it to see that you are in a different atmosphere. Somehow the very smell of the thing is different; the atmosphere, everything about it is somehow different. It is in a category almost all of its own. It is the one book in the Old Testament that is thoroughly Gentile in its atmosphere and that is why it is different. All the other books of the Old Testament are in the atmosphere of the people of God, always. But this book of Esther is a book that is thoroughly Gentile in its atmosphere. Everything in the book is Gentile. The customs are Gentile. You don't find any Jewish customs. The phraseology of the book is Gentile. It is the one book of the Old Testament (we shall find out in a few moments) that has more Persian words and phrases, more, shall we say, Gentile words and phrases than any other book. It is completely Persianised. Better, shall we say it has a Gentile atmosphere, a Gentile wording and phraseology, and Gentile customs. The whole book is Gentile to the point of shunning the things of God.

Esther is a remarkable book and I am going to be rather brutal in our whole method in study because I think we shall find that the book of Esther is anything but what is the normal perception of it. Many people love the little book of Esther. They think it is very wonderful. It *is* a wonderful little book, but it is a very wonderful little book, in my estimation, for a very different reason from what most people think. The plain matter of the fact is this: it is thoroughly Gentile. Right down to the minutest details, it is thoroughly Gentile. Even its language is not the language of the people of God. Its very language is the language of the unsaved. Its customs are the customs of the unsaved. Its atmosphere is the atmosphere of this world. If we can get that, we are beginning immediately to get to the heart of this book. It goes so far that you almost would think that the things of God are in disrepute. You would almost think that for some reason or other, there were no such things as the city of God, the house of God, the land of God, the people of God, the Word of God, and so on.

If we had only the book of Esther to go by, we would know nothing. We would not know that there was a law. We would not know that God had spoken. We would not know that there was a promised land. We would not know that there was a city, except for one little mention that, some hundred years before, someone who was the son of Kish had been carried away captive from Jerusalem. That is the only reference to Jerusalem in the whole book. We would not know anything. So we understand at the very beginning, that this book is thoroughly Gentile.

Esther's Placement in Scripture

It was on account of its Gentile atmosphere, and particularly its Gentile phraseology, that its genuineness, its place in the Canon of the Scriptures has been questioned again and again and again and again. The more thoughtful rabbis, not by any means the popular ones (I shall say something about that in a moment), but the more thoughtful, scholarly, and deeper sighted rabbis continually wrestle with this problem of Esther. What was this book doing as Scripture? It denies everything that the Jews stood for. It seemed to get right to the heart of the problem in the wrong way. It seemed to bless the very thing that the rest of the Law and of the prophets had so violently condemned. Therefore you find that the rabbis, those more deeply sighted and more studious ones, have always wrestled with the problem, "What is the book of Esther doing in the Canon of Scripture?" What is she doing there? Why is she there? Why has she been afforded such a place?

That's one side, but the other side is rather amusing. Esther, by popular esteem and acclaim, has had the highest place in the Jewish heart that anyone has ever had. It is the most remarkable thing. It is not merely that she was counted by the Jewish people and the popular rabbis to be one of the three most beautiful women that ever lived in the world. I don't think it was just the fact that everyone loves a beautiful woman. It was more, I think, the fact that somehow or other this history, this story that is contained in the book of Esther has answered something in the hearts of the people of God in a very remarkable way. It is a remarkable thing, the esteem that the book of Esther is held in, to this day, by the Jews.

The last chapter of the book of Esther tells us of the Feast of Purim, which just means the feast of lots. It has forever after commemorated the events of this story. Though at times in Jewish history, right up to recent years, other feasts have been forgotten, the Feast of Purim has never been forgotten, but has always from that day to this been meticulously observed by the Jewish people. It is not only that they have meticulously observed the feast that commemorates the story in the book of Esther, but there are many remarkable stories that the Jewish people have about the book of Esther. For instance, it was commonly believed, and is still commonly believed that in the days of the Messiah the only two things that will remain will be the law and the book of Esther. Everything else will be put on one side, but the law, that is the Pentateuch, the first five books of the Bible, and the book of Esther will remain throughout the days of the Messiah. It is only a small tradition amongst the Jews, but a remarkable one.

The Five Rolls

Another interesting thing is this: the book of Esther in the Hebrew Scriptures had its place in the third section, which is the Writings. There are: the Law, the Prophets, and the Writings. The little book of Esther is in a subsection of that division, the Writings, or the *ketuvim*, which we call the Five Rolls[1]. The book of Esther is the principal one of those five rolls: Ecclesiastes, Song of Solomon, Esther, Ruth, and Lamentations[2]. But the principal of those five is Esther, indeed it was known as *the* roll. When anyone spoke of the rolls and they said: the 'the roll,' they meant Esther. Now why on earth has the little book of Esther such esteem amongst the people of God? It is interesting isn't it?

I think it is even more instructive to note the way in which the Holy Spirit has taken it away from that section and we now have, under the government of the Holy Spirit, that it is the last word of sacred history. Isn't that interesting? The last word of sacred history. It has been removed from its position in the Writings and placed at the very end of what we call the historical books of the Old Testament. It is the final word. It does not chronologically belong there. If we were to try and fit it in anywhere chronologically we would have to try and either put it before the book of Ezra or after the book of Ezra because in actual fact, chronologically, it comes halfway in the book of Ezra. But it has been put at the end of the book of Nehemiah and it is the last word in Old Testament history.

I think we can say that we have already seen something of God's ways with those that return to the land. We have seen something

---

1 Also called "The Five Scrolls"
2 https://en.wikipedia.org/wiki/Five_Megillot

of God's dealings with them, but what about the people, the vast majority, who remained in exile and remained happily in exile? How did the Lord deal with them? How did He reveal Himself to them? What were His methods with them? Did He give them up? Did He forsake them? Did He refuse to have anything to do with them? What was the Lord's attitude to the vast majority of His people who never went back to the land, who never returned to the place where God's name dwelt, but remained happily and prosperously amongst the Jews of the dispersion? Now, the little book of Esther deals with that: the people of God who remain. God deals with those of His people who remain in exile.

The Purpose of the Book of Esther

The purpose of the little book of Esther is to reveal God's dealings, God's ways, God's method, and God's attitude to those that remained in exile. Twenty-three chapters (and I am not being sarcastic, twenty-three chapters) are given to the little, tiny remnant of some 60,000 souls who returned to the land. But of the countless thousands, running more of course into millions, that remained in exile, we have only ten chapters. Twenty-three chapters, Ezra and Nehemiah, given to those that returned and ten chapters to the vast majority who remained.

We are going to deal with the technical side; we will take it in two parts, Lord willing. In this first part we will take the technical side, and lay a foundation, a thorough foundation, for anything that we might say upon the book itself. In the next part, we will deal with the spiritual lessons. We shall find some spiritual lessons, quite a number of them actually in this first part, but we will be dealing primarily with the technical.

There is one thing I would like to say and it is this: Esther is a great corrective of the Holy Spirit to those people who are given to narrow prejudices and dogma and who in their minds restrict God to the realm in which they are, to the ground upon which they find themselves, and refuse to believe that God can be found anywhere else but where *they* are, can only bless people where *they* are, can only use people where *they* are, and can only meet with people where *they* are. It is a tremendous corrective to that narrow, earthly, natural attitude of so many of us that somehow or other, if other of the Lord's people don't see eye to eye with us, then the Lord can't be with them. He can't be for them. For many Christians, their greatest problem is: "How does the Lord bless *that*? How did the Lord bless *that*?" All kinds of weird propositions are put forward. For example, some people would absolutely swear that the Lord could never be found amongst Roman Catholics; there could not possibly be found a child of God amongst the Roman Catholics. Others will say that it is not possible for the Holy Spirit to use a Jehovah's Witness. Yet, we have proof, we can give you proof that the Lord is found sometimes in such amazing realms and can use the most amazing things. But do you see what I am getting at? We have such little minds. We have such a small capacity that we cannot conceive of the Lord being able to bless, or use, or meet with anyone unless they see the same that we see. "If the Lord has revealed this to me then it must be true. Therefore, what about all these others to whom the Lord has not revealed it? How can He bless them? How can He meet them? How can He save others through them? If this is the truth surely the Lord should be narrow. He should cut them all off, and give Himself only to those who are prepared to go right on with Him."

Now, the book of Esther is the corrective of the Holy Spirit against that kind of natural mentality on the one hand. On the other hand, it is a great corrective to those people who have that sentimental looseness and that insensitive non-discernment. You know that kind of thing. They will be prepared to be involved with anything that has been blessed. To them, so long as the Lord blesses it, that's all right. Let's get in; let's get on the wagon. If the Lord is blessing it, then it must be all right. You hear people saying it again and again—most of them will draw the line when it comes to some things, but generally speaking, their attitude is: "If there is blessing, we are prepared to be involved. The Lord might be there."

There is no discernment. There is absolutely no understanding that the blessing of the Lord does not mean the commitment of the Lord. There is no understanding of the book of Esther. This little book of Esther is a great corrective, on the one side, to those of us who cannot believe the Lord could be with anyone else except on this ground that we find ourselves on. Or on the other hand, a great corrective to those who believe in that kind of sentimental looseness: "Let's be involved with anyone that the Lord is blessing or have got a few aspects that are alike. They are the children of God aren't they? Aren't they the children of God? Aren't they our flesh and blood sort of people?"

Well, there we are. That is the book of Esther. I might say one other thing and then we will go straight on into the authorship and the date. Esther is one of the very few books of the Old Testament that is not quoted once in the New. Think of that. Esther is one of the very few, there are only literally, a very few that are not quoted in the New Testament.

Authorship and Date

Now, what about the authorship and the date? We have nothing internal or external that gives us a single clue to the authorship of the book of Esther. Whoever wrote it was minutely familiar with Persian customs, with Persian life, and with Persian court life. Whoever wrote it was obviously someone who lived in Persia because of their command of Persian phraseology. They have used a Hebrew which is thoroughly Persian. That is all we can say about it. It is someone who, not only lived in Persia, but obviously had imbibed the very spirit of Persia. Now that is very important.

We can also say one or two things about suggestions. One suggestion that has been made from the very earliest stage was that Mordecai himself was the author of the book of Esther. This has been made from the very, very earliest stage. The earliest church fathers said that they thought it was Mordecai, and before that some of the great rabbis thought it was Mordecai. The Talmud, on the other hand, has attributed the authorship of the book of Esther to the great synagogue under the leadership of Ezra. Today it is very common amongst Bible scholars to throw overboard both suggestions. Until recently, most Biblical scholars felt that the date of the book of Esther was a very late one. They felt that it was written, because of its style and its language, some considerable time after the events that it describes took place. But now, more recently, there has been a renewal of interest as to whether, in actual fact, the book of Esther was written at the time that the events described took place or just afterwards.

There are one or two reasons for this. We will not go very far on this question of authorship or date really, but there are some very interesting points which we may wish to make because we are going to draw some lessons out from them later on. The book of Esther is, as we have said again and again, much more Persian than Jewish. Of course, Esther herself, I think, was more Persian than Jewish in many ways as we shall also see. There can be little doubt that the book of Esther was originally a Persian document in the royal archive. That is the latest and, I think, the most satisfactory of all the theories that have so far been expressed concerning the sources of the book of Esther. It would explain a lot of things. It would explain its Persian phraseology. It would explain the fact that the things of God are never once mentioned anywhere within it. There are some very, very interesting points that we cannot include now. However, it would seem that, in its earliest form, it is not in the same form as we have it now. It was a Persian document from the royal archive of the Persian Empire.

Now, this could argue in favour of Mordecai's authorship because if you look at the very last chapter of the book of Esther you will find that Mordecai was next to the king. Furthermore, it would be somewhat in keeping with Mordecai's character, both naturally and spiritually, I would say. For, if you remember, it was Mordecai who counselled Esther not to let it be known under any circumstances that she was a Jewess. Do you know what that meant? It meant that Esther had to eat things forbidden in the Law of God. It meant, in other words, that she had to run contrary to all the Law of God concerning the people of God. We shall see a little bit more about that later, about both Mordecai and Esther. But you see, dear Mordecai, it would seem to be somewhat in keeping with his character, *if* it was him. Being in charge of the administration of the Empire, being next to the king in greatness, if he came to write up the record of Haman's execution, Haman's ten sons' execution, and also the very real retribution taken out upon all the people throughout the land which ran into thousands and thousands and thousands of people killed by the Jews, perhaps Mordecai would have felt that it would be wiser not to bring the name of God into it. If he felt that it would be wiser not to bring the word of God, nor the things of God, nor Jerusalem, nor the house of God into it, he might instead very carefully have expunged from the record anything that could possibly give, outwardly at any rate, the glory to God.

Well, there you are. I have my own little theory I would like to mention, but please don't take it as necessarily anything. I really wonder whether that may not be somehow the key to this book of Esther. Something in it just feels that it may well be the key to the book of Esther. Mordecai may have been behind it and I would not be the least bit surprised. According to the Jewish tradition, it was compiled in its present form under the leadership of Ezra and the great synagogue back in the land. I would not be the least bit surprised, that it was worked over by Ezra. This would also explain why in some way, though so Gentile, it has a style reminiscent of Chronicles, Ezra and Nehemiah.

You see, most of you probably do not know that a terrific row raged for years over Chronicles, Ezra, Nehemiah, and Esther, and particularly over the question of Esther's date of compilation and where it was. Modernists have always, adamantly, until recently, said that Esther was a complete fake, the whole thing was rubbish, it was just a lovely, pretty story of Jewish patriotism. Of course, now, more recently that has all changed due to archaeological discoveries and much else.

It is interesting that now there are the two sides taken. On the one side you have those who say, "Ah, but look at its style. Those Gentiles look so like Ezra, Nehemiah and Chronicles, and most do believe that those three, that three-fold work, is the work of one hand. On the other side, you have those who try to make out that because it is so Persian, it is probably an unknown Persian scribe who actually wrote the story, which explains why you do not find the Lord's name in it.

We can fix a date for the actual story, though not for the compilation of it. However, we can fix a date for the actual story because it took place between the sixth and the seventh chapter of Ezra. We are almost absolutely certain about that. That is, the story that is contained in the little book of Esther, took place between the first and second stages of the return to the land. There are something like 60–70 years between the first and the second stage of the return to the land and it was during that period that the story described here took place. It was in the reign of the famous Xerxes. In Hebrew we have the name Ahasuerus. Again, there is some discussion as to whether Ahasuerus is a title or a very poor Hebrew transliteration of the name Xerxes. He was one of the most famous of the Persian kings. We shall say a little bit more about him in a moment.

Esther begins in the third year of Xerxes' reign. That is the year in which he deposed Queen Vashti. Then he married Esther in the seventh year of his reign. In between the third and the seventh year he was on a great Greek expedition in which he was very tragically defeated. He came back to marry Esther. That is at least something of the background. The book of Esther covers a period of 20 years, approximately.

There is very little real indication of the date of its compilation. As I have already said, the language used suggests that it could have been written much later than the events which it describes. Yet there is so much detail within the work that would suggest someone contemporary wrote the events described. Ahasuerus' chamberlains, all seven of them with unpronounceable names are mentioned, which seems to be just a little bit odd a century or two later. Also, all the names of Haman's ten sons are given, and many other minute details, which would seem to be that of an eyewitness at least. Thus we have that problem again.

The Background of the Book of Esther

What about the background of this book? I hope you do not mind us spending just a few minutes on the background. I think it will shock everyone probably a little, but I think it is all the more important if we could knock some of the silly ideas and misconceptions of the book of Esther out of the picture.

The History of Xerxes

Exactly who was Ahasuerus, or better Xerxes? He was one of the greatest of the Persian kings. History tells us that he was proud, he was self-willed, he was arrogant, he was wanton, but at times he could be very merciful, very kind, and very loving. He was known through the whole lengths of his Empire for his amorous nature, which we need to underline. That side of him, I am afraid has, of course as always, been taken up very greatly in folklore and much else. Xerxes was famous on the one side because he was a true symbol of the eastern despot, an absolute potentate who could do anything at will. He was taken up because he was a famous soldier. He won the Punjab for Persia and brought it within the Empire. He was the one who conquered most of Ethiopia and he brought the Mediterranean islands into the Persian Empire. When he came at last to his great expedition against Greece, he confidently thought he was going to win, and therefore also have Greece in the nest, do you remember? But the great prophecy of Daniel concerning Persia and Greece came to pass according to the word of the Lord over these two great empires, little Greece beginning for the first time to emerge into a great, great power and civilisation.

Persia and Greece clashed under the leadership of Xerxes. It was this great expedition that he planned in the third year of his reign. He had a vast fleet. I don't know how much you all know about that, but he had a great navy, of which he was very proud because Persia was for the most part inland. He lost nearly the whole of his navy at the battle of Salamis, which turned the table forever against Persia. A little later he lost nearly the whole of his army. Those reports, although they are sometimes exaggerated, they are not in the scriptures, say 2,500,000 men were in his army when they met defeat. And although he did not lose his army, his army was badly crippled. So in the seventh year of his reign, for the first time in his life, he was a defeated man, and he returned home to lose himself in home and domestic matters. He reigned from 486 to 465 BC.

The Queenship of Esther

It has never been clearly established whether Esther was *the* queen or *a* queen. I think this is one of the things that might shock everyone, but I think it is just as well everyone knows. Ahasuerus, or Xerxes, was known to have had a number of wives. He had a vast number of concubines. To this day we are still not sure whether Queen Vashti was *the* Queen or whether she was the favourite concubine, whether Esther took the place of the favourite concubine, or whether, in actual fact, she took the throne of the Queen. If (and I am now just speaking through secular history in this background and not from the scripture) as the scripture says, she became the Queen, we still have today some unsolved problems. For if Vashti is the Queen that we know under another name, who was the Queen consort from the beginning to the end of Xerxes' life, then we can only suppose that she was deposed for a while and Esther made Queen in her place. So, you see, we still have some problems about the Queenship of Esther. I personally prefer to believe the Scripture because in every case so far, the Scriptures have been absolutely vindicated, in the end, to be thoroughly, historically accurate. There is no suggestion that she was *a* queen, but *the* Queen with *the* royal crown given to her. However, I feel that you ought to know at least something of the difficulties on that side.

What we can say is this, that Xerxes was known to be exceedingly amorous and by no means confined his feelings to the queen. That, I think, we ought to make abundantly clear. Vashti, on the other hand, was known to be a very cruel and profligate woman. Most people, and in all our Sunday school books, we are always told that poor Vashti was asked to do something that she should never have been asked to do, something very evil. She was asked to come into the presence of these drunken nobles and the king with an unveiled face. But in actual fact it was the custom in the drinking parties of the royal house of Persia to have their wives present. So it was not quite such an indecent thing as we suppose. Far from it; it was an affront by the Queen publicly to the king when she refused to go to be with him. That we also need to make clear.

In the third year of Xerxes' reign, he called a great general conference. All the nobles of his 127 provinces, all the leaders, the governors, the princes, and nobles were gathered together at Shushan, the winter palace, for a general conference which lasted quite some months, to plan the expedition against Greece. There is no doubt about it that Xerxes was a great soldier and a great strategist. He planned with his generals and his nobles and friends, very carefully and minutely, the expedition against Greece. It was at the end of that time when they had a sort of general end-of-conference feast that Queen Vashti was asked to appear and publicly affronted the king in front of all his governors, nobles, and the rest. You know the story, how from there on it became a government matter and how Vashti was dealt with.

When he went against the Greeks, he was away, evidently rather upset and annoyed, for quite some years, but at last he returned. In the book of Esther we don't find much of that, but it was in the seventh year of his reign that he married Esther. It is generally believed, and it is most obvious from all accounts, that when he was defeated and lost the campaign, when the campaign against Greece failed and collapsed, he returned to

Shushan to the palace to lose himself in matrimonial matters. That is quite clear from the long drawn out business. I am not being funny when I say that, really, all it was, was an ancient beauty contest. All the beautiful young ladies of the whole land were asked to come and there a was a general beauty contest, until one by one they were knocked out or taken to a section where at last one was chosen. If you read it carefully, you will see it lasted six months to a year. It was a very carefully planned thing. All one can say was that Xerxes was a defeated man and did not like it, so he turned his mind to other things.

The story we have in Esther took place in the palace at Shushan. It was the winter palace, as far as we know, one of the three capitals of the Persian Empire. That, I think, really is all that we need to say about the background. A lot is there, and later on we shall look at it further. When we actually read the story, we shall see quite a few other things. That's the background. That's the man that we call Ahasueras. That is something about the background, as far as we know through secular history, of the atmosphere that surrounded Esther.

I think you will all agree that this is not an atmosphere that one would have thought the Lord would have chosen for His children. I do not think any of us would for one moment think that the Lord meant us to be party to all that, really, or in many ways to be involved in it. Yet, the amazing story of the book of Esther shows us that God allowed, and indeed arranged, for some of his people to become intimately linked and involved in this very situation, in order that He might meet them, deliver them, and use them. We shall say a little bit more about that in a moment.

The Key to the Book of Esther

Now what about the key to this book? What is the key to this book of Esther? We have got a problem here when we come to this key: how to put it in a few words. Sometimes we can put in one word the key to a book. At other times we can't put it into a word at all. It needs quite a paragraph to be able to put into one word the key to a little book. It is only a little book, but how difficult it is to find a word that will describe it.

Let's look at some of the facts and then we might find the key. What are the facts? The facts are these: the Word of God never appears once in the whole ten chapters of the book of Esther. The name of God, Jehovah, never appears once. The promised land is never referred to once. It is not even implied in any statement. The city of God is mentioned only once in a reference a hundred years back, that's all and then it is not mentioned as the city of God or anything else, it is just simply called Jerusalem. The house of God is never once mentioned or implied. The Word of God, and this is the staggering thing, the Word of God is never at any single point, mentioned in the whole of this book. The Septuagint translators, the translators of the Hebrew Scriptures into Greek, were so embarrassed by this silence on everything they held dear, particularly as they were Jews of the dispersion anyway, that they elaborated on it falsely. The result is that in the Septuagint version you have numerous references to the Lord, to God, and to other things. In fact, they added quite a few chapters to the book of Esther to try and get over their very real embarrassment over the simple fact that there wasn't a single reference anywhere to the things of God in this book. Now, on the other hand, (listen to this,) in the ten chapters, and by the way they are small chapters, in the ten short chapters, the Persian king is referred to 192 times. The Persian kingdom is referred to 26 times and the personal name of the Persian king is given 29 times. That is on the other side.

Esther and Ezra/Nehemiah Compared

I want you also to mark the amazing difference between Ezra/Nehemiah and Esther. On the one side you have got Ezra/Nehemiah. Now listen to these differences because they are truly remarkable when you have them pointed out to you. In Ezra/Nehemiah everything centres in the city of God. Everything. The whole of those 23 chapters is found, in the end, to be summed up in the walls being built around the city. The very house cannot be built anywhere else but on this ground called Jerusalem. Nowhere else. When you come to Esther do you know what is mentioned all the time? Shushan. Shushan takes the place of the city of God. Everything is centred in Shushan. All the stories take place in Shushan; that's one thing.

Another thing is this: in Ezra/Nehemiah, you know as well as I do, without appearing to be irreverent you almost become tired of the repetition of the name of the Lord, "The Lord, the Lord, the Lord, the Lord." Everything is the Lord! Nehemiah cannot open his mouth without appealing to the Lord. Ezra cannot open his mouth without appealing to the Lord. Everything is the Lord! Everything is to the Lord, everything is before the Lord, and everything depends on the Lord. It is all the Lord. In Esther it is all the king. It is all Ahasuerus. The Lord is not mentioned.

In Ezra/Nehemiah, the Word of God is taught carefully. Now I do not mean it is just preached; I mean it is taught.

The people are instructed carefully in the meaning of their history and in the real meaning of the Word of God and the Law of God. In the book of Esther you do not get anything at all. Nowhere, anywhere do you find the Word of God taught in that way.

In the book of Ezra/Nehemiah everything is worship. You remember how we found everything was worship? All the way through it led up to worship. In the book of Esther you will not find the word worship, nor will you find an act of worship anywhere in the whole book.

In the book of Ezra/Nehemiah you will find that the thing they stressed all the time was separation for witness. If there is going to be any real witness there has got to be separation. Now here we are getting into the heart of the thing. In Ezra/Nehemiah look at the pains that the prophets took, look at the pains that Ezra took, look at the pains that Nehemiah took, even to plucking peoples hair out, and so on, to ensure separation! Everything depended upon separation, clearly defined, clearly distinct from everything around. Yet, what do we find with the book of Esther? There is no such thing as separation. Indeed, we find the exact opposite. We find these people are moving right into situations and seemingly the Lord is leading them. You see, Esther could never have been in that palace for those years, for those *years*, and it not have been known that she was a Jewess if she had not broken every known law of Scripture. Do you realise that? I don't think it will embarrass you, but there are all kinds of things, laws, particularly over a person like Esther that she would have had to have kept if she was obeying the law. She could not do it without it being known. But no one knew.

You see, it was only when she got Haman, the King's favourite, and the king the second night running into that banquet that she suddenly thinks when the officials had left the scene and she says, "Well, I might be destroyed." They never knew when they made that decree that she was a Jewess, yet there she was sitting there eating. One thing that divided Jew and Gentile were the laws of the food. It irrevocably divided them. We have Ezra/Nehemiah dividing everyone from all these other things. On the other side, we have the Lord using someone who is hopelessly mixed up, and the Lord seems to be blessing them. In Ezra/Nehemiah we have got poor Ezra and Nehemiah bent on one thing: divorcing foreign wives and getting rid of foreign children. In Esther we have got all the energies of Mordecai and the Lord putting Esther into marriage with a Gentile king like Xerxes.

Now, I think if Christian people were to just sit down and reflect for a few moments, they would find that they would have a key to a whole lot of situations in the book of Esther. This lovely little story, we all love at Sunday school, we should find has got everything we want and a bunch of keys for the twentieth century situation. What a remarkable thing it really all is!

The Name of Esther

Now, I am going to tell you one more thing that might shock you. Do you know what the name of Esther means? No doubt some of you know. It means a star. Do you know that that name is a foreign Gentile name and do you know what really it was the equivalent of? It was the equivalent of Venus. Really, it commonly, popularly meant *good luck*. I am sorry to shock you. You have always had such high ideas about Esther. But that was the meaning of her name. Her Hebrew name meant *myrtle*. But her Persian name meant just what we know today by the name Felix—good fortune, good luck. When you get down to brass tacks in this story and cut out all the sentimental sweetness that so often surrounds it, what an amazing picture is presented here! A child of God, part of the Persian harem is married to a Persian, Gentile despot, a proud, arrogant, self-serving, wanton man in an atmosphere which was entirely heathen. That is what we have got in this book.

It is all the more remarkable because in all the Jewish homes of the dispersion we find some rather remarkable things. For instance, gradually, idolatry was being forbidden in the Jewish homes of the dispersion, as was intermarriage; it was being frowned upon. The law of God, though not understood, was held in great respect, which is all the more remarkable. Esther draws a veil over that, but in actual fact those things were happening amongst the people of God. There is a meaning by the Holy Spirit to put the book of Esther in its present form into our hands because it is not an absolutely true representation of every Jewish family in the dispersion. Many of them were good people, many of them were devout people, but they were not prepared for the rigours of leaving for the promised land. They wanted to have, as it were, their spirituality on *that* ground. They wanted to have their salvation on *that* ground. They wanted to have their experience and blessings of the Lord on *that* ground. They wanted to remain on *that* ground, but have the Lord. So, it is most interesting if you really do look upon it, carefully, in a right way, you would see straightaway that with all of this devotion to the Lord, they remained on ground where God's house could never be built, where God's purpose could never be realised, and where God's Christ could never be brought in.

Now, you and I would immediately say, "Well, well, well, the Lord must leave them then. That's quite definite, the Lord must cut Himself off from them. If they are going to stay on ground where God's house cannot be built, where God cannot really be satisfied, where God's purpose can never be realised, and where God's Christ can never be brought in, then God should have nothing to do with them." However, that is just the point of the book of Esther, and that is the corrective that we need against this natural narrowness of the wrong kind that we have. Those children of God, the vast majority of the people of God, remained on that ground. The Lord never took His salvation from them. Not only did the Lord not take His salvation from them, but He developed His salvation. If they did not want to be where the House of God could be built, if they did not want to be where the presence of Christ could be realised, if they did not want to be where the Christ of God could be brought in, all right, they would *lose* that. They would lose it. But they would never lose their salvation. They were still people born of God and God would defend them to the hilt because they were born of Him. Do you see? They were born of the seed of Abraham. He was with them, absolutely with them.

Now then, it is in that atmosphere that the story of Esther takes place and here we are coming to the key. Everywhere you turn you will find the hidden sovereignty of God expressed toward His people wherever they are. The hidden sovereignty of God is working for His people, not so much *in* them, but working *for* them. Everywhere you look in the book of Esther, the Lord is working for them. Everywhere. It does not matter where you turn, the Lord is working for them. It is a most wonderful thing. In spite of their location, in spite of their ignorance, in spite of their compromise, in spite of the fact that they are not prepared to abandon themselves to the Lord, the Lord is working for them. Oh, how that explains so much in Christendom today. Wherever you find a child of God, the Lord is there if He can be. The Lord finds Himself in the most remarkable places *for* some of His own. Places that you and I would just put right out, but the Lord is there *for* them because they are born of Him in the most remarkable way. Furthermore He will give the most remarkable experiences to some of them.

I remember once when I was in Egypt hearing something I just could not believe. (I must be careful because I want to move on to the last point.) In Upper Egypt amongst the Copts, who were anything but what we could call born-again believers, I heard of an old, ancient woman. Two friends of mine, who were most accurate in their discernment, saw her. At times, and it was most definitely, according to the mature and aged judgment of these friends, she came under the Holy Spirit in the most remarkable way so that blood appeared upon her hand and when that occurred she was able to do anything. The most remarkable instances of healing and salvation had been recorded all over the place there in Upper Egypt. How could you explain this? You can either say it is the devil or you can say it is something else. That woman was a born-again believer. She was mixed up in the most unbelievable setup you could ever wish to see, and only those of you who know anything about the Coptic setup could know what on earth I am talking about. Never have I seen anything quite like that. But there you are. It is there and sometimes you will find the Lord in the most remarkable places.

Oh, I could go on—we come to instance after instance after instance of places where you would not expect to find the Lord working for His people, and there He is working for His people, blessing them, coming down to their level, finding them on their level, expressing Himself to them on their level, doing the most unbelievable things toward them and for them.

The Hidden Name of God

Now here you have got it all in the book of Esther. I think this is all most clearly seen in the hidden way in which we find the name of God in the book of Esther. I am afraid I am rather tired and rushed, so it is not done very beautifully, but I hope that it will be to all of you a real blessing in some ways to understand something of the fascinating nature really of true Bible study. You see, people have said for years and years and years that the name of God is never mentioned in the book of Esther. You could never find it in there until a man called Bullinger some years ago discovered in a search into the writings of the rabbis that in actual fact the name of the Lord occurred four times in acrostic form in the book of Esther.

The acrostic form simply means the first letter of each word of the sentence being one letter of the name of the Lord, Jehovah. So, in the book of Esther, four times, each one at the point of crisis in the story, you will find the name of the Lord. You will find it first in Esther 1:20, then in Esther 5:4, then in Esther 5:13, and then in Esther 7:7. In each case, you will find it in a most remarkable context.

For instance, you will find that the first two are the initial letters of the first four Hebrew words of the sentence. In the second two they are the final letters of the first four words. You will find that the first and the third are read backwards and the second and the fourth are read forwards. In every single case, they are consecutive.

Now, it cannot be coincidence. Knowing how we have acrostic psalms and other cases of this strange literary method, it cannot be coincidence that in the book of Esther, at the four points of crisis in the story, the name of the Lord should appear in a hidden way. Dr. Pierson, for those of you who know Dr. A.T. Pierson, who wrote a lot on the Scriptures, has put them into couplet form. I took his first couplet form of the Authorised Version and put it on the board[3]. You see:

Due **R**espect **O**ur **L**adies, all,
Shall give their husbands, great and small.
Esther 1:20

Isn't it interesting that those are the initial letters? In each case that the initial letters are used, it is God initiating the deliverance of His people. In each case the final letters are used, it is God fulfilling the deliverance of His people. It is read backwards, the first one, L O R D. Then the next one in Esther 5:4:

Let **O**ur **R**oyal **D**inner bring
Haman feasting with a King.
Esther 5:4

---

3 See page 279—283 for charts

That is the word of Esther when she arranged for the King and Haman to come two nights running to that banquet so that she could speak to the King about the truth.

The third time it is the words of Haman, which were overruled by God. Do you remember his hatred when he saw Mordecai at the gate? He went home and had those gallows built for him. The Lord overruled his hatred and the building of those gallows to his own destruction.

> GranD foR nO avaiL my state
> While this Jew sits at the gate.
> Esther 5:13

And lastly, the words again of Haman when he saw that his end had come:

> IlL tO feaR decreeD I find,
> Toward me in the monarch's mind.
> Esther 7:7

Although I think what A.T. Pierson wrote sounds rather funny in some ways, he has done a marvellous thing for those of us who don't understand Hebrew. We can understand what exactly lies in this history. Here we have got at least in some degree or form something akin to what the Holy Spirit has written in the book of Esther. The name, not of God, but the name of Jehovah, the name of the Lord, appears four times. The chosen name of the Lord, the name by which he revealed his relationship to his people comes four times in this story.

8.
The Sovereignty of God in the Book of Esther

You will remember from last time that the last thing we said on the question of the key to the book of Esther was that it was the sovereignty of God, in a hidden way, working for His people. The rabbis used to say that God was not among His people in the book of Esther; He was for His people. It is true to say that the teaching of the book of Esther is simply this: it reveals to us that there is one realm in which God works in a veiled way for His people. There is another realm in which He works in a revealed way to His people.

We would define it, perhaps to the shock of some, in this way: the first realm we would say is the realm of Christendom, or the Christian realm. God works in that realm in a veiled way. It is all things. It is experiences of God, truly of God, but only experiences—things, teachings, doctrines and so on. In the other, it is a realm where we are immediately, and from the beginning, brought into a direct relationship with the Lord Himself over which

He is terribly jealous. This will mean the complete devastation of ourselves in order to bring us into a real knowledge of Himself, and of His purpose, and of our destiny in Him. That is what we call the church realm. It is a realm where we are truly being built up into Christ as members of His body.

So, the book of Esther does reveal to us that there are clearly two distinct realms in God's dealings with His people. Notice that we are not talking about the world. We are speaking of His dealings with His people. In those two realms, God operates on very different principles. We find in one realm (that is back in the land, in the city) He is getting people to divorce their foreign wives. In the other realm He is arranging for Esther to marry an evil, Gentile king. In one, He is seeking to separate His people from every contaminating, foreign, Aryan influence for the very value of their witness depends on their separation. But in this other realm we find the Lord Himself blessing people who are, as a principle, hiding the fact that they are children of God. We have to understand that for Esther to live in the palace for a few years before she revealed the fact that she was a Jewess meant that she more or less had to eat food that was forbidden. She had to follow customs that she could not possibly have been involved in if she was obeying the Word of God—the law of God. So, we have these two different realms. Now, we must go on with the outline of the book.

Outline of the Book of Esther

You will see in the chart straightaway what the outline is. The outline of the book of Esther is a very, very simple outline.

It falls really loosely into a division of three, at least that is how I have seen it and I have put it just simply like that. The first division is the sovereignty of God determining things before the event. That is the first two chapters of Esther. Then, from Esther 3–5, it is the

> **Esther Outline**
> 1. The Sovereignty of God
>   a. Determining things before the event or crisis
>   b. Esther 1–2
> 2. The Event or Crisis Itself
>   a. The annihilation of God's people planned and timed
>   b. Esther 3–5
> 3. God Sovereignly Intervening
>   a. Turning evil into deliverance and salvation, honour and glory
>   b. Esther 6–10

event itself, the annihilation of God's people planned and timed. Lastly, from Esther chapter six to the end of this book it is God sovereignly intervening and turning the evil into deliverance and salvation.

So, let us look at this book of Esther. If you will, turn straightaway to the first chapter. I want you to keep continually before you all that has been said previously about the background and the sphere of this book. It is very, very important that we should remember that. How God reveals Himself in this little book of Esther would answer a thousand and one queries that we have as to how God blesses a lot of things in the Christian realm.

One of the greatest problems among Christian people is: "How can the Lord bless *that*? How can He use *that*?" For instance, take this question. Someone says, "The Lord has shown me that you ought never to ask for money. Now, how does the Lord bless such-and-such an organisation, and such-and-such an organisation, and use them to save other people, to bring other people to Himself, if they go round from door-to-door collecting? Or another, perhaps they make big appeals, or they advertise in some Christian magazine. I don't understand it. If the Lord reveals to me that this is wrong, and that I should not do it, how does He bless that?"

So you see, in our human way we have a thousand and one queries about why the Lord blesses so many things, why He uses so many things, why He is found in so many strange atmospheres, societies, institutions, and so on. When we read in His Word what He clearly wants and when we are walking with Him, He begins to show us absolutely clearly how we should walk. Do you see? Well, the book of Esther is the answer to that. It is an Old Testament book, but in type it very, very, beautifully, simply, and clearly gives us a bunch of keys to many, many problems that we have about Christian work and activity.

The First Division—God's Sovereignty Before the Crisis

Let's look now at the first of these divisions in the book of Esther, the sovereignty of God determining things before the event or the crisis. That is, God, in His sovereignty, prepares things long before the crisis boils to a head, long before it. It is a great comfort to really look into this book and to discover something of God's gracious sovereignty on behalf of His people.

The Story of the Book of Esther

First, I am going to tell you the story. We will cover the story and any points that need to be cleared up. Then we will draw the lessons from the story. So now, what is the story that we find in the first two chapters of the book of Esther? The book of Esther opens in chapter one with this great conference being called. You will remember that this great conference was one of the greatest conferences called in that generation. It was a conference of all the civil and military leaders of the Persian Empire. At that time the Persian Empire extended to 127 provinces. From all these provinces, the civil and military leaders were brought together for a conference which lasted approximately six months. There was a tremendous amount of spade work to be done over those days. The purpose of the conference was to plan the great Greek expedition. Xerxes or Ahasueras, as we know him here in the book of Esther, wanted to plan an expedition against Greece to bring Greece itself within the orbit of the Persian Empire.

You will remember how all were gathered together, and it began with a feast only for leaders; that was a big banquet. We know from history the Persians did an awful lot of their business at banquets. It was an official way of doing business. The banquets lasted often two or three days. Some have been known to last a week, when you hardly ever left the room. You reclined there eating on and off and talking and discussing. That was the way business was done. It began with a feast and then after six months there was a final feast. The final feast was for all the people as well. It was not just the leaders, but the representatives of the people were also brought in on that. I think it is a most remarkable picture of the luxury, the wealth, and the opulence of the Persian court that we find in this first chapter.

If you read chapter one in the Revised Standard Version, you will find a very, very simple but wonderful picture of the Persian court: all the hangings of white cotton and blue, which were the Persian royal colours. (Green, by the way, as far as we can see at present is a Persian word, that is, a Sanskrit word used here in Esther. Its Hebrew meaning would be "green," but most scholars think it much more probably means cotton because it is a Sanskrit word for cotton.) Then you find the wonderful description of the pillars. By the way, archaeologists have discovered intact the very pillars which we are thinking about here, upon which great awnings hung. There were gold and silver couches that they sat upon and gold and silver vessels that were used. We know from history that the Greeks captured quite a number of these things. So, you see, the Bible is not exaggerating these things. It is a very clear picture of the luxury of the Persian court.

We just do not know what this wonderful pavement is of red and white and other colours. The Revised Standard Version translates it as mother-of-pearl, porphyry, and so on. However, we do know that with the Persian Empire, a pavement in the palace was something sought after to be the thing. So, we have an amazing picture of a remarkable court, and indeed in some ways, a somewhat remarkable King, and a six-month conference beginning with a feast and ending with a feast.

It was at the final feast for the people that ended and terminated the conference that the King sent, via his chamberlains, for Queen Vashti. All he wanted her to do was to appear with her crown on. Of course, we know that the record says he was a little bit "merry," but it was quite the thing done in the Persian court for the wives to be present at these banquets in which business was discussed. Therefore, it was not a base or a lewd thing that he was asking Vashti to do, but just simply to come in for the final part of the feast wearing her crown. For some reason that we do not know, Vashti refused and of course that was a public affront to the King in front of all his leaders and the people as well. When the chamberlains came back and said that Queen Vashti had just sat down and refused to come, evidently it must have caused a pretty big stir.

It is true of the character of Ahasueras as we know it, that he became exceedingly angry. It was not a personal matter, it was made immediately a government matter and he put it into the hands of his statesmen. It had just been suggested that there was some friction between Vashti and the seven leading statesmen that controlled the court who very, very swiftly wrote, in the King's name, a decree which divorced Vashti and deposed her as Queen. They said, quite rightly, that if this affront became known throughout the whole Empire, as it obviously would, then husbands everywhere would be treated with contempt by their wives. That was something that they felt was something they had to nip in the bud. So, the decree was made and Vashti was deposed. Now it may all seem a rather remarkable story. However, the whole point is that behind all this was God.

You will then know, if you go on to chapter two, that there was a rather remarkable beauty competition, which is the only way to describe it. All the fairest and loveliest maidens that could be found were brought to the palace and carefully selected so that from them the King could choose his new Queen. What the story does not tell us is that quite some years had passed between the divorce of Vashti and the choice of Queen Esther as the new Queen.

You will also note that "Esther" is a Persian name which means *star*. It is very akin to the name we know as Venus, and in Persian it just meant *good luck, good fortune*. She was considered, and the

Hebrew stresses it doubly, that she was thought to be exceedingly beautiful. She had lost her father and her mother and she had been brought up by her cousin Mordecai, who brought her up as his own daughter.

Then you will note that we are told another remarkable thing. In the family of Mordecai, there were two names which are rather remarkable: Shimei and Kish. These evidently were his father and his grandfather. Yet, as the rabbis have pointed out, these names have always recurred and recurred in a family pedigree. It is very likely that both the Shimei and the Kish mentioned here are the great ancestors of Mordecai, which is rather remarkable to say the least. Kish of course was the father of King Saul, and Shimei was famous for his cursing of David the day that Absalom rebelled against him. So there again, you have a rather remarkable background.

You remember that when Esther came, she was selected as one of the girls in this competition. I do not know what word we can use for it. It seems awful to call it a competition, but it was a competition. I think we have got to strip the book of Esther of a lot of its sort of Sunday school atmosphere that has grown around it and see it as it really is. I might just say that all these girls that were selected never left the King's harem. They all became concubines, but only one was selected as Queen. So, Esther was selected to be part of this.

One of the things we note, is the counsel of Mordecai when he told Esther that whatever she did, she should not mention her kindred or her roots. He told her whatever she did, just to keep quiet, which meant a lot. It meant that she had to get involved in all kinds of things that were a contradiction to God's Word and God's law.

Then again, we see another strange thing. The keeper of the harem, the chief of the King's harem, immediately favoured Esther. For some reason that we shall never know, naturally, except for later being explained as the sovereignty of God, he favoured Esther. Of course, it was in many ways in his hands to make or break any of those girls' opportunity to become Queen. He so favoured Esther that he advanced her. He put her very near the top, and indeed it would almost seem by implication that she was really, very, very greatly favoured. Then of course, you know the story that when Esther goes to the King, the King chooses Esther as Queen.

However, these two chapters end with something else that is also somewhat remarkable. They end with the story of Mordecai sitting outside the King's palace and overhearing a plot, which he tells Esther about and she in turn tells the King. The King has the whole thing investigated. It is found to be true, and the men are executed. That is all that we are told at present, but you see that is the story behind these two chapters.

The Sovereignty of God Behind the Scenes

Now, what are the lessons that we can learn from these two chapters? The first is this: the sovereignty of God lies behind the whole scene. Here you have got worldly rulers. They are despots, absolute Oriental potentates and dictators in a way that we could not conceive of or believe. They are men who could, in a minute, order the destruction of thousands upon thousands of people. That is the atmosphere. You have a court that has been and is to this day, famed for its opulence, its luxury, and its wealth. Seemingly, everything is absolutely in the iron-like hand of the court. Worldly affairs, worldly rulers, everything of this world and yet, behind the whole thing, the sovereignty of God is using the world like pawns. God is taking a man, even like Ahasueras, and using him as a pawn. He is taking all the affairs of his very government and using them to achieve His own ends. It is true, it is absolutely true, that there are world rulers of darkness, but there is an even greater and more remarkable truth about human history: behind the very darkness of human history stands God Himself. The very story, the very events of human history are being overruled and woven into achieving and realising God's own purpose.

Here you have a most remarkable story! God is here sovereignly, in a hidden way, but He is there. You do not find His name mentioned as such, you do not find Him spoken of, you do not find Him referred to or deferred to, but He is there. This is one of the most wonderful and the most remarkable facts today, something that many of our brothers and sisters are being called upon to experience: that in some parts of the earth where despots reigns in a reign of bloodshed and terror, they know that behind it all is the sovereignty of God, who can use the despots like pawns to achieve His own ends. They think that they are contradicting God, they think they are destroying the work of God, but in the end, they will have been found to have served God's counsels and His ends. That is a remarkable thing that is clearly revealed here in the book of Esther.

The Sovereignty of God Arranges the Circumstances

Another lesson that we learn is this: long before the event takes place, long before the crisis boils up, we find the Lord counteracting, planning His counteraction, planning His deliverance of His own. Take this divorce of Vashti. Do we believe the Lord is in divorce? Well, of course most of us would immediately say, "No," but this was one divorce the Lord was in. This was no mistake believe you me. Whatever you might think about divorce, the Lord engineered this particular divorce. If Vashti had not been divorced there would have been no Esther, there would have been no deliverance of the people of God. They would have been wiped out, man, woman and child. Do you see what the Lord is doing?

Now here some will have great questions, shall we say reverently, on the morality of God. How does He do something that He reveals is manifestly wrong? Well, that is a problem that you will have to solve; I am not going to talk about that. However, I am going to state the fact that if the Lord had not engineered the divorce and the deposition of Vashti, there would have been absolutely no answer in the coming days. Years before it took place, years before the crisis boiled up, the Lord, as it were, deposed Vashti. I wonder what exactly it was, if I may use rather crude, colloquial expression, that 'bit' Vashti that day that she was asked to appear before the King and his leaders. Something. It may have been a very, very small thing (as so often is the case, small things lead to big issues), but there was some reason why she just suddenly decided she was not going to go in. But whatever it was, the Lord was behind it. So you see, this is something remarkable.

The Sovereignty of God and Esther's Selection

I might say that Esther's selection is also a remarkable thing. That a Jewess could be hidden and be selected was a miracle! But I think it was even more remarkable the way the Lord, as it were, influenced the chief of the harem. Is the Lord for harems? Somehow, I don't think so, and yet here we have the Lord working on the leader, the chief of an Oriental harem. Furthermore, He so works and influences him that he favours Esther. If you read the story with an unbiased and unprejudiced mind, you will find that he had a lot to do with Esther being chosen.

Then, you remember another very remarkable little thing. They were allowed to take anything they wanted when they went to the King. They went in the evening, you see, and came back in the morning, and they were allowed to take anything they wanted. It is remarkable because it says Esther took nothing. She left it to the chief of the harem. He told her what to take. That may seem a small thing, but the advancement of Esther by that man was a gain due to the sovereignty of God. You see Esther might have wondered what it was all about. The fact was that she had been selected to be in this competition, as it were, and whatever happened she would have been a concubine of the King for the rest of her life. She might have wondered what on earth it was all about. Why, why, why? She had no idea of the crisis that was some years ahead in the future. No idea at all. So again, we find the amazing sovereignty of God bringing a Jewess to be Queen of the Persian Empire.

Last time we spoke of some of the difficulties that we have, historically, over this particular portion of the Word of God. However, we are standing firmly upon the Word of God itself, even if it opposes history as we have it. One thing we can say here is simply this: we know from history that no woman was ever chosen to be Queen to the Persian King who did not belong to the seven chief Persian families of the nation. That she should have been selected and chosen to be Queen was a miracle in itself, and far greater the miracle that she was a Jewess.

You ask me: What can God do when His people go into exile, and you find them under the heel of an evil, heathen, Gentile nation? What does He do? He raises up one of His own people to be Queen over the whole situation. That is the sovereignty of God. Oh, you will have many questions about it. How could the Lord possibly have allied her to a man like Ahasueras? How could He have possibly allowed her to be involved with all the court of the day and everything else and be a child of God? It is something that we might well scratch our heads over and ask many questions about. But the whole point is this: the sovereignty of God is expressed in the book of Esther by the way that a Jewess becomes queen of the whole Empire. Well, there we are.

I might also say the sovereignty of God was in Mordecai's discovery of the plot. What a remarkable thing it was, that he should just have been there and overheard those two eunuchs, those two chamberlains discussing together in their anger what they were going to do to King Ahasueras. What a remarkable thing! Oh, we might say it was just a little incident. Mordecai told Esther. Esther told the King. The King immediately started an investigation that ended in finding that the matter was true and two men were executed. That ended that plot very swiftly. Actually, Ahasueras *was* assassinated. That was how he ended his life, but *that* plot of assassination ended. But the remarkable thing is, that this was the sovereignty of God again.

Later on in the story, the King couldn't sleep one night and he asked for the records to be read. They dug up some of the records—how on earth they ever dug up those records—but there again is the sovereignty of God. When they were reading the records, they suddenly discovered that a man called Mordecai saved the King's life some years previously. You remember what happened. The King said, "What has been done for Mordecai? I can't remember doing anything."

They said, "Nothing has been done been done for Mordecai"

"What? I must do something straightaway."

So, you see the sovereignty of God and the point at which the King discovered that nothing had been done for Mordecai, was the point at which Mordecai, though he did not know it, was at his greatest danger. Gallows were actually being built the night the King could not sleep—50 cubits high. Of course, there we have another problem. They were 70—90 feet high, those gallows that were being built. All through the night the work went on building those gallows. The King could not sleep; not because he could hear what was going on, but for another reason. But the whole point was this: do you see the sovereignty of God in every single step? Mordecai did not know. Esther did not know. Far less did Ahasuerus or any of his statesmen or court know. None of them knew. They were all being brought here ... put there ... woven together by a hidden hand that as yet they did not see. Do you see? That is the sovereignty of God working in a most remarkable way behind the scenes.

God's Sovereign Grace

I want you also to note another lesson from these two chapters connected with these other two. If God in His sovereignty is behind world events and behind world rulers, (whatever they are, you can't get beyond God), and if in His foreknowledge He is planning His counteraction long before the event takes place, another thing that we ought to note is that God's sovereignty works because of His grace. We can call it sovereign grace in the foreknowledge of God. What do we mean by that? God is working in His grace for His people in His foreknowledge in spite of their condition and their compromise.

We would have said, "The Lord should have left these people. They have no business to be there. They should have been back in the land. They should have been back in the city of God. They have got no business to be there in exile."

However, although the Lord knows they are compromised, although the Lord knows that they would not leave the exile and go back to where they should be, although He knows that they are right out of His purpose in that sense, as far as the coming of the Messiah is concerned, yet He works in His grace for them. Now that is another wonderful thing. You see, we often cannot understand why the Lord works in the remarkable way He does in the Christian realm—how He saves people, how he blesses them, how he uses things, the experiences of deliverance and provision that he gives in the Christian realm, in all kinds of things that we would consider to be wrong, foundationally wrong in some cases. Yet there you are; you find the Lord. Why is it that you find the Lord? You find the Lord in His sovereign grace is there. In spite of the compromise, in spite of the condition, wherever there is a soul that cries out to Him that is His own child, He is there. So that is something that we ought to take note of from this book of Esther.

Then I want you also to note following from that, that here we are taught God uses things, He takes hold of things, He plans things that He would never touch in the Land. He would never touch them. Just supposing the folk in the Land, back in the promised land had been in terrible need. Do you think He would have taken one of those men who had a foreign wife and used him? Oh no. The Lord was spending all His time and energy divorcing them through Ezra and Nehemiah. You know the trouble they had to get the breakup of families to try and wipe out that kind of thing. But here, we find the Lord is using the very thing He is condemning. In the land He is condemning it, and He is condemning it in no uncertain terms. He is dealing with it in very severe and harsh terms. But here He is arranging it. He is using it. He is taking hold of the very thing He condemns. Now, do you see? You cannot involve yourself in just anything that is being blessed in what we call the Christian realm. Just because it is being blessed does not mean to say it is right. God blesses a tremendous number of things that are compromised in different aspects, but He blesses them.

From this we are taught simply that the Lord works for His people just because they are His own. Just because they are His own, He will not forsake them; He will not leave them.

So here we have these remarkable opening chapters of the book of Esther. God is really working for them. It runs right through the whole book. Don't you think that is rather remarkable? I think it is a tremendous corrective to our confused, muddled thinking about the Lord's people today. Do you see?

The Second Division—The Crisis Itself

Now, what about the next bigger section of Esther? You find that it is all concerned with the actual event itself. We have been dealing with things before the event, the sovereignty of God working toward it. Now we have the event itself related. What is the event? It is the complete annihilation of the people of God—man, woman, and child we are told. The decree is made that every man, woman, and child of the Jewish people should be destroyed.

What is the story in these chapters 3—5? We find a man called Haman the Agagite. Now isn't this interesting? Haman the Agagite. Who was Haman the Agagite? Well, evidently somehow or other He is related to the Agag we know of. Do you remember, how Samuel hewed him in pieces? Because Saul refused to take action, Samuel was angry, do you remember? The kingdom was taken from Saul in the end over that. Do you remember? Now isn't it strange? Mordecai is linked with Kish, is linked with Saul? On the other side you have got Haman and He is linked back in history with Agag. Isn't it strange?

Then you will find some other rather remarkable things. This Haman is the King's favourite. (I know that is a rather remarkable things to say.) Mordecai, and we don't know why, refused to bow down to him. Now, no one knows why Mordecai refused to bow down to Haman, because one thing that we don't find in the Old Testament is any restriction upon showing deference and respect to superiors. So, we have no idea why Mordecai refused, except that evidently he felt that it was something to do with being a Jew. Which is all the more remarkable when we consider that Mordecai had told Esther to keep quiet. So here we have a little problem. Why didn't Mordecai save an awful lot of trouble and just simply bow his head and flatly bow his body as Haman went by? But he didn't and that was the beginning of the trouble.

It was reported to Haman, first of all, of course. Mordecai was asked and Mordecai gave the reply that he was a Jew. So the servants went and told Haman and Haman noted it the next time and was exceedingly angry. But, being a vindictive man, he said he would not take it out upon Mordecai only, but he would destroy the whole race of which Mordecai was a member. So we have the remarkable plot to destroy the Jews. They thought to cast lots. It is no haphazard thing. They cast lots. By divination they come, after many, many months, to the point where they know that it is to be a certain date. It is to be the thirteenth day of the twelfth month. They found that out by casting lots, by divination.

When Haman knew the date, he went to the King. I suppose it was something about nine months hence, and he laid the plan before the King. He persuaded the King to take action saying that these people were dangerous, and the decree was made. Now, that was the master stroke of the devil because a decree made by the Persian court was irrevocable. It was one of the strongest, most stern things about the authority of the Persian court, that any royal decree was absolutely irrevocable. So, the decree was made on the thirteenth day of the twelfth month. Every man or woman who wanted to get rid of the Jews was absolutely given the right to do so. So that on that day, there would be a bloodbath throughout the whole length and breadth of the Persian Empire.

The reaction of Mordecai is interesting. For the first time we see, although it is not actually mentioned by words, that he prayed.

It says he went out into the city and cried with a bitter cry, evidently fasting in sackcloth and ashes and so did many of the other Jews throughout the land. Esther becomes exceedingly concerned. She sends some clothes to him. She evidently does not like to see him in that condition. However, he sends them back. The result is she sends a message to ask what on earth is wrong with him; he sends back to her word of what is wrong. She then says, "Well I can't do anything about it." Evidently, she felt she had fallen just a little out of favour because she said. "For thirty days I haven't seen the King" and just wondered whether it would be more than her life's worth to stand before him.

Now she was a clever woman, Esther, because you see, she had the right to ask for an audience. But if she'd asked for an audience and it had been refused, she could not ever mention that matter again without losing her life and she knew that. So when the word came back from Mordecai, "How do you know, that you have not come to the kingdom for such a time as this? Do you not realise that if this does happen, you will also lose your life." It is a law of the Persians and the Medes. It has got to be carried out. It will go right up to the top of the land and right down to the lowest strata of society. Then we get those wonderful words of Esther: "I will go in to the king. If I perish, I perish, but I will go in. But you spend three days in fasting and in prayer and I and the girls here will spend three days in fasting and prayer." So they all wept and waited on the Lord for three days.

You know the story, Esther went in and in a wonderful way, the golden sceptre was held out to her. She had got her wish. Now, Esther was a very clever woman. She was not only a very beautiful woman, but she is revealed in the story as a very,

very clever woman. She did not ask straightaway, which I think was a very wise thing on her part. She said, "Would you like to come to a meal?" You know the story. They came to the meal and you know Esther's success.

Satan's Hatred of All God's People

What are the lessons we learn from this part of the story very simply? We learn this first of all, and I want you to understand this. Satan's bitter hatred of all God's people even when they are not where they should be, even when they are compromised. Now do not make any mistake about this. Satan hates the seed of God. He *hates* the seed of God. Many Christians make a terrible mistake when they think of going back into the world. Everything is rosy, everything is beautiful, everything looks wonderful when you go back into the world. I have not known a backslider who has not had moments of real joy and gaiety when they have gone back into the world—at the beginning. But then suddenly, when they are absolutely chained in the world, the devil reveals himself for what he is, and they lose everything that they ever had! They lose their health, they lose their mind, they lose their peace, they lose everything. Oh, if only the people of God would realise that once born of God, Satan will never rest until He has destroyed the ones of God.

You see, you must not think that the devil is breathing sweet little things into your ear and saying, "Come on my son; I'll give you a good time. You come with me. I want you, I want you. I like you. You come with me, you'll have a good time. No more going against the current. No more of that awful trouble. No more of the pressure of the Christian life. No more of this wearing nature. You just come with me, and I'll give you a wonderful time."

You just go with him and you *will* have a wonderful time. For a season. The devil will see to that. He will give you a wonderful time for a while. You will have whatever you wanted, and then you will discover that you are manacled. You are absolutely shackled in a way that you were never shackled before. You will discover that you are in the presence of the most insidious and the most violent hatred. Malice is the only word to describe it. It is not God. Oh, the devil breathes it into your heart when you are in such a position that this is God's anger, but it is not God at all. You are in the presence of someone who is out to destroy your very body because he cannot destroy what is of God.

That is what Paul meant when he said he delivered two people over to Satan for the destruction of their bodies, do you see? Satan would be only too pleased to destroy their bodies. He cannot touch the seed of God, but oh, how cruel—he will torture and he will torture and he will torture a child of God. Now if you want any proof of that—oh, if only some of you could go and see some backsliders, real backsliders, people who have really been born of God. You see them years after they have gone back and see what it has done to them, see the incredible marks, the scars that are upon them. Now, why? You would have thought that by going back into the world, the devil would just love it! You would have thought that he would have patted you on the back. Don't you deceive yourselves! There is something in you that is born of God and Satan hates it and he hates you. He hates you! If you step out of Christ, you will have a wonderful time for a while, but then you will discover that you are absolutely in a place of unbelievable burning. Torment.

Oh, people don't believe these things. God wrestles with them. He pleads with them. He beseeches them to come to an understanding, but they feel the other side until too late. But then, when it's too late they are right back. Oh yes. Do you think Satan loves God? Think again. You go home and just ask yourself a question, "Does Satan love God?" Then ask yourself another question, "Does Satan love what is born of God?" Then you have got your answer to what would happen to you or to me if we step into his hands. He will destroy us. He will destroy us ... not swiftly, but unbelievably slowly. So that is what we find here.

You will note here something else. Satan hates the people who are walking in Christ, and he hates those that fall away from Christ, those who are not walking in Christ. I believe that Satan hates those who have abandoned themselves to the Lord on certain ground, but he also hates those who are not on that ground. That explains an awful lot of Satanic conflict that many places and organisations have. He hates everything that has anything of Christ.

Satan's Plans

I want to say something else in this: Satan's plans are never haphazard. They are always planned and timed. You think you are walking into something, you think you are doing something, you think you are yielding to some coincidental temptation, but you are doing nothing of the kind. The whole thing is a carefully made plan. It might go back years, but it is a plan that has been laid, and it is a plan that has been timed. I have never yet known any person who has really fallen; fallen in a way that meant backsliding, that has not been at a point where it was planned and timed; the exact point of time carefully planned years before. The devil never lays coincidental plans. They are not just hap, not haphazard. The devil's plans are carefully laid and planned, carefully timed, just like this plot in Esther.

I want you also to note that the anguish and the travail are not so much over the Lord's name and over the Lord's honour and purpose. You remember Mordecai went out and wept with a bitter cry and so did all the Jews throughout the Empire. But I want to ask a question. Was their anguish and travail over the name of the Lord, or the purpose of the Lord, or the honour of the Lord, or the glory of the Lord? I am sorry that I have to answer that it is not. Their bitter cry was that they were going to die.

Now that reveals something that is only too common in that realm. It is all "I" and "we." There is a realm of Christianity in which everything is judged on what you get. If you don't get enough here, you go where you do get enough. Do you understand what I mean? You can leave anything if you don't get enough there and go somewhere where you get more. Everything is what you get, what you get; you judge everything by what you get—whether *you* are satisfied, whether *you* are getting something, whether *you* are content, whether *you* get fellowship, whether *you are* happy, whether everything suits *you*. It is that kind of spirit. Well, I am afraid it is here. The thing that stirred these people up to cry to the Lord was not the Lord's name and honour and glory or purpose, it was simply that it was the very point where they were going to die! Well, anyone would cry to the Lord in such circumstances, I might say. I am not being unkind. Mordecai's a great man and

Esther's a great woman of God. But we have got to see clearly that here we do not find them praying for any other reason than the fact that they are driven to their knees in prayer because they are going to die. Their anguish, their travail is a result simply of that.

So, I might say that we learn something else. In God's sovereign grace, He has those at such a time who are there appointed by Him and who are comparatively faithful. If we were to compare Esther with Nehemiah and Ezra and others we would say, "Well, these are nothing" But you see, comparatively speaking they are the faithful in exile. The Lord always has such ones at points of great trial for His people. Church history, the history of the people of God down through the generations, is marked by this kind of thing. Some tragedy is taking place, some terrible thing is looming up and a handful of comparatively faithful people—in their generation they were the most faithful in those conditions and in that atmosphere—gave themselves to the Lord, abandoned themselves to the Lord. Then what happens? You find another page of Christian history is written of the tremendous deliverance of God. That is just like church history. All throughout Christian history, you find it again and again.

We note also on this question of this event, the annihilation of God's people planned and timed, we learn this very simple thing, that the Lord waits in His sovereignty, although He is sovereign, He waits until His people are reduced to crying to Him. Now this is an amazing thing! If you read Psalm 107, you will find that although God is absolutely sovereign and could deliver His people, He never does. He waits until they are reduced to crying to Him. When they cry, He hears their cry and lifts them up. Isn't that a remarkable thing? If you read Psalm 107 in the light of Esther, you will be very surprised, I feel, to find how the Lord deals with His own. He reduces them to the point of utter need until they cry out from the depths of their hearts.

Well, those are lessons that we have learnt here. We will take the last portion next time. We want just to simply learn from these two great divisions of Esther. God in His sovereignty is working for His people long before the event takes place. Wonderful plan! Next time we shall see how the Lord actually intervenes when the event is about to take place. We shall discover some very wonderful things. We shall discover how the Lord takes the very thing, the very things that Satan is using with the desire of destroying the people, and He uses those very things to destroy the enemy. Gallows are being built? Who hangs on the gallows? The man who built them. So that is just like God in the finish. Sin? Who will be destroyed by sin? The devil himself. In the end, sin will have destroyed him but the Lord, by the coming of sin, has saved us.

These are amazing things. The sovereignty of God behind things, planning toward things and then when they are about to take place ... intervening. It is a wonderfully comforting thing that the Lord is never, ever taken by surprise. Have you ever thought of that? Well, think about it again. The Lord is never taken by surprise. Isn't that wonderful? There is not a thing that the Lord does not know about that happens and there is not a thing that He has not planned. You may be on the right ground, you may be not on the right ground, but if you cry to the Lord you find the Lord has all the provision there, planned, ready, prepared, waiting.

That is really something of the story so far of the book of Esther. If there is anyone being tempted by the enemy to go back into the world, take note of what I have said, because what I have said is not just theological or theoretical. It comes from real experience in some measure, and even more from observation of what has happened in so many lives. We are hated. That is why things are so difficult. We are hated. Never think that by getting out of the sphere of the church that you will be less hated. You will have only jumped, as it were, out of the frying pan and into the furnace, into a place where you stand to lose everything but your soul.

There are some words I thought I would read to you, words that are nearly always quoted when it comes to the book of Esther. I do not know why because they were not actually written about the book of Esther but they were always and everywhere written. I thought that I would read them to you and leave them as the closing thought:

> *Careless seems the great Avenger;*
> *history's pages but record*
> *One death-grapple in the darkness*
> *'twixt old systems and the Word;*
> *Truth forever on the scaffold,*
> *Wrong forever on the throne,*
> *Yet that scaffold sways the future,*
> *and, behind the dim unknown,*
> *Standeth God within the shadow,*
> *keeping watch above his own."*

9.
The Remarkable Message of the Book of Esther

Now, will you turn to this sixth chapter of Esther? Remember previously we spent our time upon the first two divisions of the book of Esther. We have already spoken upon what we have learned from the book of Esther. We know it is the most Gentile document in the Bible. It is the most Gentile in atmosphere, the most Gentile in phraseology, and the most Gentile in custom. Because of its almost Gentile origins and the fact that it hardly mentions the things of God, the city of God, the Word of God, the law of God, the name of God, the word God, and because it hardly mentions anything that we are accustomed to in the rest of Scripture, its place in the Scriptures has often been questioned, both by the Rabbis and by the early church fathers.

I think we have begun to discover that when we strip the book of Esther of so much of the earliest conceptions of it, we have one of the most remarkable stories. In some ways, until we find the key and the message of this book, we find here one of the most remarkable problems in the whole Bible. We find in the Bible that the vast rest of Scripture which both precedes and succeeds the book of Esther, spends its time and is at much pains to teach us and to instruct us in certain principles of God. Yet, the book of Esther seems to contradict what the rest of Scripture teaches. Indeed, not only does it seem to contradict it, but it would seem to suggest that God is very, very much *in* the contradiction. That is the problem of the book of Esther. Ezra and Nehemiah spend all their time divorcing people—foreign husbands and foreign wives—sending them back to their countries, whereas the book of Esther shows us that God here is found arranging the marriage of Esther with one of the most profligate of the Persian kings.

We could say much, much more about the book of Esther. It is a most remarkable book! When stripped of so much of our Sunday school conceptions of it, when we get right down to business (which I am afraid very few Christians have really been able to do) it is remarkable. For instance: when you look at some of the commentaries on the book of Esther, you see the lengths to which commentators go to get around some of the difficulties which are really almost funny. They are frightened to death of really facing the truth that is so unfortunately stated by the Holy Spirit Himself! Then again, for those of you who would like to look at it, it is even funnier when you take up the Septuagint version of the Old Testament and read it there. You will be amazed at the changes that were made when the old Jewish scholars, the old Jewish rabbis, in Alexandria some 100–200 years before the Lord Jesus was born, came to the translation of the Old Testament into Greek. The Greeks of the Exile found it so embarrassing that this book did not mention the things of God and so on that they decided there and then to make up for the absence. The result is that in the Septuagint we have a very, very elaborated version of what we have here with the book of Esther. That is something we cannot spend more time on, otherwise we should need another study on Esther going back over everything, much as I would like to do that. As you know, the basis of teaching is reiteration and some lessons we can learn only by the thing being reiterated and reiterated and reiterated until at last, somehow or other it gets into us that it is right, that it is there.

Well, here you have got the book of Esther. It is the last word in the record of sacred history. That is, with the book of Esther, the divine record of Old Testament history is at an end. There is no more record of history now until the days of John the Baptist. This is all the more interesting, that we should have found the book of Esther at the end of Old Testament history. Chronologically it does not belong to the end; Nehemiah belongs to the final end. But here we have the book of Esther.

The Two Realms

We have found that the book of Esther teaches that there are two realms. God's people are divided quite distinctly in the mind and in the eyes of God here in the book of Esther in a natural, geographical way into two clear cut realms. One we call the Land, the other we call the Exile. What God does with His people in the Land is entirely different to the way He reacts to and the way He rules and the way He governs His people in the exile. This is the most remarkable fact of these three books: Ezra, Nehemiah, and Esther. We find that God seems to have two entirely different sets of rules. He deals with His people here in the city, in the Land in an entirely different way to the way that He deals with them there.

Now, you will remember the first study we took on the book of Esther, we were at great pains to show in the book of Esther how entirely different it is in every single way. This is what the world has taken up and flung at the Christian through the centuries: how God seemingly contradicts Himself. In the same era of world history, He is doing one thing there, and the exact opposite here. He is teaching one thing there, and the exact opposite here. He allows this there and rules it out here. There it has the severest penalties attached to it. Here it has not only not got any penalties attached to it, but the Lord Himself is arranging it. How strange! You, see? No wonder people in the world have flung this at us as being inconsistent. But within that very, seeming contradiction there is the key to the whole problem.

God's Sovereignty Before the Crisis

Well, we have found that the book of Esther is divided into three. The first two chapters of Esther deal with and teach us the sovereignty of God determining things before the event. Do you remember how remarkable we found that? In this realm, the realm of the Exile, God is there in a hidden way. He is for His people, but not among His people. He is not revealing Himself; He is there in a veiled way. You remember again in the first study, we discovered the name of God in acrostic form at four points in the Hebrew text in this book. It is a most remarkable fact. The name of God is not mentioned once in the whole book of Esther, yet it is there! It cannot be coincidence that it is there.

There are far too many remarkable things about those acrostics that rule out any coincidence at all. It is there by design. What does that teach us? It teaches us that in this realm God is present in a veiled way, in a sovereign way. Thus, we found that the key to this book is the sovereignty of God, or the sovereign grace of God, however you would like to put it.

The problem it deals with is the problem we face today. Why does God use some things? Why does He bless some things? Why does He take up some things? Some of us would say, "The Lord has led me along certain lines; I could not possibly ask for any money." Yet we know some organisations that appeal for money, beg for money, and the Lord seems at times to greatly bless them and use them. Then we say, "Wow! If the Lord has led me this way, that cannot be right! Yet the Lord seems to lead that and bless that." We can give a thousand and one illustrations of this problem. Why does the Lord take such great pains to lead us along *that* path, to teach us that this is right? To not allow *us* to go back, otherwise the most severe things seem to happen. Yet, just across the way as it were, you find the exact opposite—the Lord, seemingly blessing, using, taking up and so on, when we cannot understand it. Why, why, why this seeming contradiction? Well, here we have it: the sovereignty of God determining things before the event. Here in this realm, there is a tragedy about to take place and long, long before ever that tragedy comes to its enaction, we find that the Lord is counteracting, determining it.

Quite a few people have asked me about what I said previously about the Lord engineering the divorce of Vashti, but it is a fact. I am not saying the Lord is for divorce at all by that, but He certainly engineered the divorce of Vashti. You have got the most remarkable fact that there the Lord is engineering the circumstances that lead to the deposition of Vashti in order to make way for the enthronement of Esther. Even if He did not, the whole point remains that Esther married a divorcee in that matter. You see, it is a strange thing. It all seems so wrong, doesn't it? But there you are; we are onto something. We can put it that way. The Lord is determining these things before ever Esther, Mordecai, Ahasuerus, or anyone else knew, even Haman did not know what he was going to do at that point. He had no idea what he was going to do. But long before the events take place everything is being shifted, everything is being worked out.

God's Sovereignty During the Crisis

And then the second point we found was in the chapters three, four and five, the next three chapters of Esther, we found the event itself is described. The event in this connection in this book, is the annihilation, the complete annihilation of the people of God. The plan was very carefully laid and timed. At the exact date the decree was made, which of course being a royal Persian decree it could not be altered or changed, it was made, and everything was settled. It was going to be the complete annihilation of every Jewish man, woman, and child. It had been perfectly, beautifully planned and timed.

God's Work of Deliverance

We note some big lessons then from these two divisions of the book of Esther. We learned, first of all, that God in His sovereignty is found in this realm working long before things happen for the deliverance of His children wherever they are, whatever their condition, however ignorant they be, just because they are His own people. Now, if we could only get free of our own limited narrowness which moves out any child of God unless they see what we have seen, or unless they are on the ground that we are on. God will deliver any child of His, in any realm whatsoever, in Christendom or outside of Christendom, just because they are His children.

It has always been so, that everyone has shut out everyone else. Whether it has been the Puritans who shut out the Quakers, or whether it was the Anglicans who shut out the Methodists, or whether it was the Protestants who intended to shut out completely the Roman Catholics. Whatever it is, you will find that there has always been this exclusiveness to some degree in the whole realm of Christendom as such. However, the point is this, and there are facts to prove it, however uncomfortable they are when people face them, whatever their prejudice is, whatever their bias is, whatever their preoccupation, the point is this: we can show you that the Lord is found in some of the most remarkable places and in the most remarkable organisations on this earth. Really.

I wish sometimes that Brother Nee had really told us a little bit more of some of the things he had seen and investigated. I think some people's eyebrows would have shot up. They would have been very, very, very surprised that you could find Christians in such a thing as this, or in such a thing as that, but they were, and the Lord will meet those people. He will provide for them, He will bless them, He will bring them into gracious experiences of Himself just because they are His own people. So, if we can only learn that we have learned one of the biggest lessons we can learn. You cannot get involved in everything which has been blessed. You cannot go and involve yourself in anything if the Lord is not leading *you* in that way. He may not be leading you that way. You can commit spiritual suicide, as it were, in getting involved in such a thing.

You see, that is the problem. On the one side, if we do not see eye to eye, we shut them out; or the other is we get involved in anything that is being blessed, or anything that seems to have some experience of the Lord, some spark of life. You cannot do it. The book of Esther is our criteria. It is our great yard stick, really, for every situation that we can find. Do you see the point? On the one hand, absolute unity in the sense that the Lord is with every child of His wherever they are found just because they are His seed. That is all. (Good old Quaker word—His seed, the seed of God.) Just because they are the seed of God, He is absolutely loyal to them and absolutely faithful to them. He will not forsake them and will not let them go! On the other side, just because the Lord will not let them go, does not mean we can join forces with them, nor does the Lord join forces with them. He is for them, but not necessarily among them. So, there is the biggest lesson we can learn from that.

Satan's Hatred for the Seed of God

Another lesson we have learned is simply that Satan has a bitter, bitter insidious and undying hatred of the seed of God. It does not matter whether they are on the right ground or whether they are off the right ground, whether they are compromised or whether they are backslidden. Satan hates the child of God and to put that into any more vivid language I cannot do, but to use the word 'hate.' That is all. Satan's hatred is unbelievable.

Many foolish Christians, as I have said previously, think that if they go back into the world they will get onto the right side of Satan. They think that he will give them a wonderful time, pat them on the back and treat them like good friends, be their friend. Don't you believe it! For a while, Satan may seemingly do a lot of things and may mollycoddle those that are on the way out or on the way back or going into compromise, but he is only doing it with one aim: to destroy with the vilest venom anything that is of the Lord Jesus there. If you could only see some of the backsliders we have seen that have been literally smashed up and torn apart, you would see Satan hates the seed of God! He will destroy a person physically because the Lord Jesus Himself said that he cannot touch the spirit. But he will destroy everything else he can lay his hands on if he can; he hates the seed of God so much.

Here in the book of Esther is evidence for it. The people of God are right out of God's will, right out of God's purpose. They do not affect the coming of the Messiah. They were not part of building the house of God in which God's whole heart and purpose centre. Yet you see, Satan hates them and he is planning their complete annihilation just because there is something of God in them. You see it is a most remarkable fact and we have to learn again that very, very big lesson.

The People's Cry to the Lord

The other lesson is simply this: when the people cry to the Lord, I am afraid it is not because they are concerned about His honour or His name. They are concerned about their preservation. But mark it, the Lord answers their cry. He will always answer the cry. In fact, He will reduce His people in that realm to crying, then He will answer them. Revivals have again and again been just this simple thing. That is all. God absolutely, sovereignly, in the most wonderful way answers the cry of His people out of reduced circumstances. When they have been brought right down to absolutely nothing, people have cried to the Lord and He has met them always and will always. It is the most remarkable thing. The book of Esther is the story of the most remarkable movement of the Spirit of God upon His own to deliver them, to save them, and to lift them up into a new sphere of service. All in exile. All in exile. What a remarkable thing it is! So, you see, we have learned some very big lessons.

God's Sovereign Intervention

Now we come to this great point of the story where God sovereignly intervenes and turns the evil into deliverance and salvation. God sovereignly intervenes. You remember last time, we were taking first the story and then the lessons. Well, what is the story of the intervention of God? I think you will remember it quite simply if we run over it. The first thing in the last chapters— chapter 6 to chapter 10, is the story of the honouring of Mordecai. You remember what happened.

Last time, we left them all having a banquet. Do you remember? There was Haman, and the King, and Esther. You remember, Esther was very wise; she did not make a petition then. She said "Look, I have one petition. It is simply this: will you come back tomorrow night and have another banquet, have another big meal with us?" They said yes, they would. Haman went home and he was absolutely elated. Just think of it! He had been lifted right up to the highest position in the realm and now he had been asked to dine with the King, the emperor of the Persian Empire alone with the Queen and had been asked again for the second time to dine with the King and the Queen alone the very next day. He went home very elated. He saw dear old Mordecai at the gate. Mordecai still refused to get up, still refused to bow. It was this that had begun all the trouble and it infuriated him.

He went home and he began to recount everything to his wife and to all the friends that were there telling them all about what had happened, no doubt they wanted to know all the details. Exactly what was there, how much they had eaten and everything else about the surroundings. He began to tell them the whole lot and at the end he just mentioned his hatred for that man Mordecai. He said, "As I left, that man did not even stand up. Here am I, dining alone with the King and the Queen, and that man still refuses to acknowledge me as his superior."

So, the story goes that they talked with him and said, "Well, why not make some gallows? You are in such favour, obviously, that tomorrow … what is Mordecai to the King? All you have got to do is, when you go tomorrow, just say to the King you want Mordecai hanged as you think he is a menace, and you will have it."

So, all through the night. Now mark here: the dramatic nature of this story is quite remarkable. All through the night those gallows were erected. Those gallows, believe it or believe it not, were something like 70 feet high. Later on, ten people were hanged on them at once. So they must have been pretty high. In fact, in the Feast of Purim the Jew has always had a star, each one to mark the ten sons that were hanged, the position of each one down the gallows. Rather gruesome, but there you are. They have commemorated it ever since and to this day they still commemorate it.

The point of the story as far as we are concerned is this: those gallows were being made all through the night in Haman's garden. You know what happened. In another part of the royal city the King could not sleep, a somewhat remarkable thing we might think, that he couldn't sleep! No doubt he tried every single means of getting to sleep, but he could not sleep. As far as we can make out from the story, he tried to sleep and he tried to sleep and he tried to sleep, hour after hour drifted away until finally he thought: "Well, the best thing to do is to have something read to me." It is a rather strange thing that he asked for the Chronicles to be read to him. While they were being read to him, suddenly, I suppose roundabout the dawn of the day, they came to this point of Mordecai. In the last study about Mordecai we read that he had overheard while in the gate a plot being hatched to assassinate the King? How he had mentioned it to Esther? How Esther had intervened? How there had been an investigation? How it had been proved correct and how those two men had been hung? Mordecai had never received any reward whatsoever or any recognition for his services. When the Chronicles were read out and they came to this heading, the King just simply asked if anything been done for Mordecai and nothing had been done at all. Evidently, according to the story, not much else happened except that the King heard someone in the court, asked who it was, and it was Haman. Haman had come to ask that Mordecai be hanged upon the gallows that he had already made.

Haman was second to the King. When the King asked him in, he just said to Haman, "Haman, what would you do to the man that I would like to honour?" Naturally, when self is in charge, we always take everything for ourselves. Not a thing, even the most harmless thing could be said against ourselves. We are either being sort of stroked or admired, or something. Anyway, Haman thought it was himself. So he falls very beautifully into a trap prepared by God. Haman begins to say what he thinks should be done, obviously thinking of himself. You can imagine it! Thinking of himself riding in pomp, the King's greatest prince leading him ahead everywhere and so on. Then, the whole of his very castles crashed to the ground. The King said, "Now, you go do *exactly* what you said, and don't leave *anything* out of what you said, to Mordecai the Jew that sits at the gate."

The King had no idea that Haman was there to ask that Mordecai might be hanged on the gallows that had been being made all through the night. But there you are; truth is stranger than fiction. You know the end of that story, how poor Haman had to do all this to Mordecai and lead him through the streets shouting before him, proclaiming before him, "Thus shall be done to the man whom the King delights to honour."

The Plot Revealed

The next thing we find about this story, of course, is the banquet. This is all the more remarkable. Poor Haman no sooner gets home, recounts everything to his wife, than the chamberlains are waiting there with something to carry him to the court, back to the banquet. He goes straight into the banquet, and you know what happens. At the end of the banquet Esther suddenly says, "Now, about that thing I wanted to ask you. You asked me to tell you yesterday so I want to tell you now." Then it all comes out into the open. She reveals for the first time that she is a Jewess. She reveals for the first time what is happening to her own people and then the King begins to get angry about the whole thing. He says, "Who on earth would dare to lay a finger on you?" Of course, in the dramatic nature of the whole story, she suddenly says, "This man." That was the end.

Well, we know from history that Xerxes was given to the most terrible fits of rage. It is one of the remarkable little incidents that showed the authenticity of the story that the King, instead of dramatically getting up and kicking the man out, was so full of rage that all he could do (because he could not control himself) was to go out into the garden into the cool. That was all he could do. But the King's servants knew full well what was going to happen. That is quite obvious because when he came back you know it says they were already putting something over the face of Haman. They knew full well when the King was angry like that it was the end for the person with whom he was angry. So, the story goes that the servants mentioned to the King that Haman, and the King still evidently did not know why, had built very big gallows in his garden. That was quite enough for the King, "That's alright, hang him on them." So we find that the gallows that Haman had built to hang Mordecai, he himself was hanged upon. What a remarkable thing it all is!

The Day of Destruction

Then the story goes on to the King's former decree. If you look to chapter 8 and 9, you find there the story moves very swiftly. You see, here is the problem. Just get this clearly, because it is very remarkable. You see, a decree had been made by the King and sealed with the King's seal. According to Persian law, no decree made by the King and sealed with his rings could ever be altered or amended. Now, the decree made was that on the 13th day of the 12th month every Jewish man, woman, and child would be annihilated. Or should we put it this way? They would be at the mercy of any who wished to annihilate, destroy them, and take their property. In other words, it was like an open check. The King just gave leave to all his subject- peoples to do what they liked with the Jew. The Jew was, as always, the most prosperous element and factor in the life of the Empire. So of course, greedy eyes had looked toward Jewish property and Jewish things and planned for that death.

Now, here was the problem: although Haman was hanged on the gallows that he had built for Mordecai, no one on earth could change the decree that had been made. That was the problem. You have got Haman out of the way, but what could you do about the decree? It was impossible. Even history itself teaches us that one of the oddest things about the Person Empire, particularly about the Persian court, was the fact that it would not change any one of these laws even when a stupid one is made. Everyone suffered. It was a remarkable thing! So now Esther and Mordecai were presented with one of the prickliest problems and difficulties that anyone could ever have had given to them. How do you amend, change, or counteract something that by law you are not allowed to change or amend or counteract?

The King, because Esther wept before him, gave her his ring. When he found out who Mordecai was and what he had done for Esther, he put Mordecai in the place of Haman. He gave to Queen Esther the whole of Haman's property. Now, Haman was a very wealthy man. It can be seen by the fact that he was prepared to pay for the annihilation of the Jews almost a third of the income of the taxes of the Empire. He was an exceedingly wealthy man. The whole of his property was given over to Esther. It was the policy in the Persian Empire, when a person was executed for a crime to confiscate his property. That was handed over to Esther. Mordecai was in the place of Haman.

Now they started to think, "What do we do?" Then they issued a decree. They told the King about it, they got his assent to it, they sealed it with his ring, and the decree was proclaimed. It meant there was another decree that could not be changed. This decree was simply a very clever one I might say. Every single Jew in the Persian Empire, on the 13th day of the 12th month was at liberty to defend himself, his property, and his children. That was all. That was sufficient. With Mordecai as the equivalent of the Prime Minister and Esther as Queen, and it known throughout the Persian Empire that she was a Jewess and he was a Jew, that was all that was needed.

Support for the plot to murder every Jew melted away rapidly, and indeed, if you read the end of chapter 8, many people became Jews. All over the Empire people became Jews, Jewish proselytes. Furthermore, all the officials of the government and administration threw in their lot with the Jew. The result was that although the first decree could not be changed, now it had been completely counteracted. When the 13th day came of the 12th month, of course as is so obvious, it was a day of terrible rioting and bloodshed. The point was that the Jew was allowed to defend himself and he *did* defend himself. He was helped by the local officials everywhere to defend himself. But this is the point: the day of their destruction became the day of their triumph. The day when they would have mercilessly been wiped out became the day when they came to a position of eminence and honour. The result was that those who had such an undying antagonism for them died that day.

The last two points in these chapters, chapter 9 and the very small little chapter 10, deal with just this. First of all, they deal with Mordecai's greatness. The greatness, the prosperity, the honour of the Jew. The Jew came to take a place in the Persian Empire at the end of Xerxes reign that was remarkable. Mordecai became greater and greater and greater. The man waxed greater and greater. Then it also tells us there was a feast established. It was called the Feast of Purim or simply, the word "Purim" means *lots*. The Feast of Lots goes back to the way that Haman found out the exact time to destroy the Jew. You remember they cast lots day after day, month after month, until they settled on a certain day for their destruction. This Feast of Purim was established then and has been kept rigidly ever since by every good Jew.

For two days the 14th and the 15th day of the 12th month in the Jewish calendar is still to this day kept as the Feast of Purim to remember the remarkable deliverance in the days of Esther.

God's Direct Intervention

That is the story, now what are the lessons? What real lessons can we learn from the story? The first lesson we learn is this: God in his sovereignty knows the exact point at which to intervene. He never intervenes early. He never intervenes late. He always intervenes at the exact point when it is most likely to be effective. It is most interesting in this story. Whereas, we have seen God in His foreknowledge working before the event ever came to pass to counteract it, He never intervenes until the point of utmost danger being reached. I suppose you would call it utmost danger; wouldn't you think? If all through the night gallows were being hammered up and put into position, all through the night they were going up, huge great gallows while there was that man Mordecai probably peacefully asleep little knowing that by morning light he was meant to ornament the gallows. That is what was happening; it is a remarkable thing!

That Lord never directly intervened until that night and that night He would not let the King sleep. There is no doubt about it at all. The Lord was there Himself to keep King Ahasueras awake that night. He did not sleep. Even with the approach of day, with every kind of modern thing to put him to sleep, yet the Lord kept the King awake. The word is simply, "His sleep fled from him." It *fled* from him! It just went; he could not find it. Whatever he did, he could not find it. The Lord kept that man awake. The whole deliverance of the people of God depended on the sleeplessness of the King and keeping the King sleepless. You know, if the King had been kept awake for a few hours and then drowsed off to sleep, all would have been lost. It was because the Lord kept him awake for so long that in the end he said, "What is the use of it? Let someone send me to sleep." As some dear commentator once said, "Nothing like some boring chronicles to send anyone to sleep." Can you just imagine it? Some courtier sitting by, droning on and on and on, of all the things. I mean it is rather amusing, isn't it? When you think of all the things for the King to ask to be read to him, whether it is humorous or not I have not the faintest idea. I would not be the least bit surprised if there isn't a little bit of divine humour in that. It always did seem a strange thing to me that the King should want to hear that kind of bedtime story. It just does not add up that at anywhere in the world, at any particular point in world history, someone should want some dry and dusty civil service document taken out and read. But obviously the poor man wanted to get to sleep. As I said probably the intonation of some half-asleep courtier droning it out was the best way he thought he could do it. But it is just the Lord's way for the deliverance of his people. Keep the man awake until he got desperate and then read the most unlikely thing that you would have thought anyone would have read to get them to sleep. There it was, it was just that point.

Now I have no doubt about it that there must have been dozens of documents that could have been read to the King, but one was selected. It was one that went back 12 years—another remarkable matter—12 years. Now if there was a diary kept, which we know there was, of day-to-day happenings in the Persian court, just imagine the remarkable nature of picking out one particular part of that journal, those chronicles that dealt with the one particular point at which Mordecai had been instrumental in saving the King's life. Yet, it was taken out and it was read to the King because he could not sleep. So, in the early hours of the morning there he was listening to something that had happened 12 years previously or so and nothing had been done about it. What a remarkable thing!

I think that teaches us our first lesson. This is the first point in the story of Esther when the Lord directly intervenes. Here it is. He directly intervenes. We learn a tremendous lesson here: the Lord knows the exact point at which to intervene for his people. It does not matter whether they are on the right ground or off the right ground, whether they are compromised, backslidden, or where they are. The Lord knows the exact point at which to intervene. The exact point. What a wonderful thing that is for us in prayer, not only for our own situations, not only for the situations for God's people wherever they are found, but even for those that are compromised or backslidden. What authority we have in prayer when we really, really consider the truth of this book. The Lord knows. He has planned for it. He has worked for it. Why do you think He allowed Mordecai to overhear that plot being hatched 12 years earlier? This was the point to which it was heading. The whole remarkable thing, all the Lord's sovereignty in action behind the scenes, before ever it happens and now suddenly it was as if the Lord stepped onto the scene Himself. He steps in and the whole thing begins now to unfold.

I tell you, the Bible is more thrilling in some ways than these modern murder stories, when you really read it with an unbiased mind and without all the unfortunate background that sometimes we have which has dulled the whole thing. What a thrilling thing it is! With just a few hours to go, here comes Haman into the court with one object, to get Mordecai hung on the gallows he has made. I say, it is the most remarkable thing, isn't it?

God's Sovereignty and Man's Cooperation

Then another lesson we can learn from this story is this: the delicate balance between God's sovereign working on the one hand and man's cooperation on the other. This I believe is one of the problems that has always filled Christian's minds from the year dot. How do we tie up God's sovereignty and man's will? How do we tie up God's sovereign working and man's cooperation? Does God need man's cooperation? God does not need man's cooperation in one sense, He doesn't. But the remarkable thing is, He never moves without man's cooperation. Isn't it remarkable?

Here in the story, you find God is sovereignly working without relation to any man or woman, long before events happen. It has all been worked out, but suddenly at one point in the story ... Esther comes. What would have happened if Esther had not gone in to the King or risked her life? Do you remember our last study, how she went in and risked her life? What would have happened if she hadn't? You remember her famous words, "If I perish, I perish." It took courage. She knew full well what a king like Ahasueras would do if she got on the wrong side of him—it would be the end of Queen Esther. She knew that. I think it is the most remarkable thing. It teaches us the remarkable nature of God's sovereign working and man's cooperation.

See how it all works out? I mean, Mordecai could not do anything about the gallows. I wonder whether Mordecai ever knew what those gallows were for, if he saw them. Certainly, he heard the hammering. He must have wondered what was going on in Haman's back garden. Little did he know what was happening. Yet later on, we find the Lord is using Mordecai. Do you see? It is this delicate balance I cannot put my finger upon where exactly the balance is, but there is a most remarkable link between God's sovereign working and man's cooperation. It is most remarkable. It is there. It teaches us it. Do you see?

You remember Mordecai's famous words, "You may have come to the kingdom for such a time as this." That is it: "For such a time as this you have come to the kingdom," said Mordecai to Esther at the point of great crisis. "You are here in this place for such a time as this." All God's sovereignty is behind it and yet it seems as if God Himself is putting Himself into the hands of frail flesh and trusting it.

I never forget that is one thing that Mrs. Fischbacher left with me two or three times. She said that at times she has thought it is as if God was putting Himself bodily into the hands of a man or a woman and trusting them with the biggest issues possible. Sometimes (and I might say the Old Testament history, New Testament history, and church history prove what I say), the whole of God's eternal purpose hangs on the finest and thinnest thread. That thread is a man or a woman. Have you ever thought about that? It is a remarkable thing! If Abraham had not gone out, what would have happened? You and I would not be here, that is the point. You perhaps do not realise that you would not be here if Abraham thousands of years ago had not gone out, not knowing where he went; we would not be here.

Again and again, I could show you where the whole of divine history hung on the slenderest thread. Oh, what remarkable things! Take church history. How thrilling church history is really when you look into it! You take a man like John Wesley, how the whole of England's future, really in one sense, was hanging on that one man and his companion Whitfield. It is as if God Himself puts Himself into the hand of frail flesh and says, "I'm trusting you with the biggest issues possible." That is God's sovereignty and man's cooperation. God does not need to do it. God does not need to do it. As dear Mordecai said thousands of years ago, "If you do not do it Esther, someone else will. If you do not do it, relief will come from another quarter. But somewhere the Lord will find one person and into their hands he will put everything as if everything depended on them. A remarkable fact!

Destruction Turned to Triumph

Then I want you also to note another great lesson that we might learn about this last division of the book of Esther. This to me is one of the most thrilling things about our salvation and about the Bible—the way in which God always takes the very thing that causes the trouble and *by it* works deliverance. Have you ever thought of that? It is the most remarkable thing! I am talking about everything that is so remarkable. But *it is* so remarkable. It is the most remarkable thing the way the Lord takes things.

Well, look at this story. Just look at this story. Haman is the instrument the devil is using to wipe out the people of God. Haman is the instrument that the devil is using to wipe out Mordecai. Very well, the Lord takes Haman, and he makes Haman the means by which Mordecai is honoured. When Haman came into that court that day the last thing in his mind was the honour of Mordecai, the glory of Mordecai. Gallows were in his mind for Mordecai, but the Lord used the very mind, the very pride, the very evil in Haman—that proud, arrogant, self-centred spirit. The Lord used *that* to plan and to work the very honour and glory of his child Mordecai. Now, that is what God does. In the end when the books are open, world history will be seen to be just like that all the way through. The thing that has caused so much trouble was the thing that God has taken hold of and through it has worked His own deliverance.

Haman built some gallows. What a remarkable thing it is, but Haman is hanged on his gallows. Do you see? He is hanged on his own gallows that he built for Mordecai. God takes the very thing that caused the trouble to work the deliverance! Haman is out of the way. Well, that is one of them gone anyway. He is right out of the way and how has he gone? He has been hanged on his own gallows. He signed his own death warrant more or less, fool that he was to build those gallows. That was the end of him. You know that has always happened. The psalmist said: "He has fallen into the pit which he himself has digged." Oh, the words of the Psalmist! How true that is, again and again! Another lovely old word in the Psalms says, 'his violence shall come down upon his own pate' (Psalm 7:16). Remember that one? I always used to love that—came back upon his own pate. Sin is just like a boomerang; it comes back.

You see, really, what a remarkable story this is. It teaches us this amazing principle that God takes the very thing that caused the trouble to work the deliverance. But you go farther on; a royal decree is proclaimed for the destruction of every Jewish man, woman, and child. Very well then, by no other means than by a royal decree will their preservation be established. It is the same thing again. One thing for their destruction, the same thing for their preservation. The same seal of the King on his finger that sealed their destruction was the same thing that sealed their preservation. What a remarkable thing it was! The 13th day of the 12th month, which was meant for the destruction and annihilation, became the day of their triumph and their honour.

You see this principle working out right the way through. I wish we could spend a lot of time on this because it is such a wonderful thing. The Bible takes it up everywhere. By woman sin came, therefore by woman came the Lord. Sin was the thing that destroyed this world. Very well then, by becoming sin, the Lord Jesus would redeem the world. It was flesh that brought the downfall. Very well then, the Lord Jesus is revealed by becoming flesh. The Lord becoming flesh. So you can see this remarkable thing all the way through, every single point of it. Where man fell, is where God caused man to triumph, in the same way and with the same conditions.

I remember when we started these studies in the Bible, we took the first three chapters of Genesis and if I remember rightly, we spent a little time upon this very thing. On one side you find the very thing that had brought the ruin of the world before the world, is the very means that God sovereignly takes up to work its redemption. Now, only God could do that. Only God could do that. Many foolish people say, "Why didn't the Lord pack the whole thing up and begin all over again?" Because God is so wise, He can do things like that. It is far, far the best to get down to the mess and then out of the mess to bring back order. Then what has He done? He has got a creation then which has learnt by its misery to never again go that way. It has learnt by it. Do you see what I mean? That is why the Lord Jesus is the wisdom of God and the power of God. The wisdom of God. His way is not our way, His thoughts not our thoughts. But do you see how wonderful God is? Oh, it is wonderful really! The way our salvation goes right down to the very points at which we fell.

So, I think there you see something wonderful in this story of Esther which should be a great help and encouragement to us. The very things that cause the trouble are the very things that God uses to bring honour, prosperity, and increase to His people. Isn't that wonderful? Never be afraid of the devil's assaults because God will always turn them, if you depend on Him and cry to Him. He will always turn them in the end, even if you have been at fault. Once you have confessed and you turn to Him, He will use those things to bring honour, prosperity, and increase. Every time. This is the book of Esther. What an atmosphere! What an atmosphere! The oriental harem, a profligate court, an evil, Gentile administration, and the people of God there contradicting everything they have ever known about the Lord God. Yet—yet—the Lord steps in and saves them. He not only saves them, but He leaves them in a position of honour and prosperity. Well, let us learn these things.

Real Experience of the Lord

What do we learn then from this last division of the book of Esther? We learn this: it is possible to have a real experience of the Lord, of His blessing, of His provision, of His deliverance—real experiences of Him—in that realm. You see how easy it would have been if we had been there in those days and we had gone back to the Land, left everything, become like pilgrim fathers, and journeyed across thousands of miles of desert to go back to the Land. Imagine what we would have thought about those people that stayed back there prospering. They were very prosperous. We would have thought, "Well, they are not worthy to be called Jews. We, a little minority, a remnant, we have turned, we have given up everything. We are afflicted. Look at us." When they got back, they had to turn a ravaged land into something of beauty. They had to build cities that had been razed to the ground by fire. Do you see? Then they would have thought of those people back there with their businesses, back there with their wealth, back there with their influence, and everything else. How very nice it was. I don't know how many of them must have thought to themselves: "The Lord cannot have much to do with them." That was the beginning of the trouble you know between the Jews of the dispersion and the Jews of the homeland, what we come to call the Hebrews and the Hellenists. This great controversy began with both trying to exclude the other.

Well, we do the same today. They might have said, "Well, they have got no experience of God." However, the Holy Spirit thinks that they have, and the book of Esther has been put into the Canon to forever underline the fact that they are God's children. Because they are God's children, God will never forsake them. Never! Furthermore, not only will He not forsake them, but they can have the most real and vivid experiences of God and of everything to do with God—of His provision, of His blessing, and everything. They can have it. Esther teaches us that. You could not have a more vivid experience of God in one way than the book of Esther tells us, could you? Face death one night and be delivered the next morning. But isn't that just what we face today?

This last division of this book teaches us simply this: in His sovereign grace, God makes His own to be great, to be influential, to be prosperous in that realm. He does. In that realm He will lift up people to the highest places, the most influential places, and the most honoured places. He will. Just as He had Esther at the very top, just as He had Mordecai at the very top, so even today He can do the same, and does do the same in that realm. It teaches us simply that there are two distinct realms, and we really have to learn that in that realm there can be real experience of the Lord's blessing, provision, and moreover, very real advancement. But, and here's the "but," and we must say it without seeking to be censorious in any way but state a fact in Scripture. Esther, Mordecai, and the whole lot of them there in Exile, had no bearing whatsoever, *whatsoever*, on the coming of the Messiah. It is one of the great facts of the Bible. If Esther had died, if Mordecai had never lived, or if they had all been annihilated in one day, it would not have affected the coming of the Messiah. The Lord Jesus would still have come when He came, and we would still be here today ourselves. Now isn't that a fact? Reflect on it, that is all I ask you to do, just pause and reflect on it.

In this wonderful realm, it simply means that here God is sovereignly working. Here He is long before the event, determining things and counteracting it. Here He is intervening at this point of time. Here is all of Satan's terrible antagonism toward these children of God, and yet though they are prosperous, though they are influential, though they have been delivered, though they have an experience of the Lord, they have not one foot of bearing upon the coming of the Lord Jesus. Why? Because they are not in the only place to which the Messiah can come. That is the lesson of this book. I believe that is the greatest corrective that we need. It comes from the very first study we took on the book of Esther. On the one side is the narrow dogma and prejudice outlook, which would narrow God's working down to our own life and time, and on the other side is that foolish, sentimental non-discernment, which will get itself involved in anything which has been blessed. The book of Esther is here to teach us just that. God is for them, God gives great experiences, God delivers them, God saves them, God provides for them, God makes them prosperous, and yet, what is the last word? What is the ultimate word? The ultimate word is they had no bearing on the eternal purpose of God. They were not an integral part in the coming of the Messiah. That is the last word.

What is the message of the book of Esther? The message of the book of Esther is a remarkable one. Here, everything that we have been taught in all the other books that we have studied so far, is contradicted. Not only is it contradicted, but we find that God does not merely allow contradiction, He blesses it. God not only blesses them, but He also uses them! I do not think I am going too far when I say God arranges them. Wow! That is the book of

Esther. There are a few more contradictions in the book of Esther that are not so easy to speak about in public. However if you look, you can see a few more contradictions. They are there.

Well, well, well, well. So, this is the message of the book of Esther. What a strange thing. What is it? If you get down to the reason why God blesses and uses contradictions in the book of Esther, which He absolutely severely judges in all the other books, you have got the key to the whole problem. You have got the key to the 20th century as well. You have got a key to the whole thing— the contradictory and complex situation is explained by the book of Esther. It just simply reveals that there are these two realms: one is the Land and one is the Exile. What God does in one, He does not necessarily do in the other. How He deals with you in one, is not how He deals with you in the other. The principles that govern one are entirely different from the principles that govern the other. How the Lord reveals Himself to you in one, is not the way you will find the Lord in the other. They are two entirely different realms. What the Lord would never touch in one, He touches in the other. What He would never bless, but judge and remove in one, He takes up and arranges in the other. Can you understand that? No wonder some people scratch their heads and think, "Can this really be the truth?" But if you study this, you will find it to be absolutely true. I have no fear whatsoever that the more deeply you study it, the more you will find that it is absolutely true.

Well, then what does this mean? What *does* this mean? We can never make what the Lord blesses, what the Lord uses, and what the Lord even arranges in the Exile, the criterium for the Land. Never. You will honour the people of God. You love the people of God. You can pray for the people of God. You can watch them being blessed and being used. You can watch the Lord arranging it. I have no doubt about it.

Years ago, when someone came forward and said they had been called to such and such a society, some people used to say to me, "I cannot believe the Lord would call them to *that* society. It can't be. It just couldn't be." But you know, when you went to the person and talked with them, you could only sit down and say, "Well, I do not know what has gone wrong, but this person has definitely been called to this weird society."

Well then, what has happened? What the Lord does there, you cannot make the criteria for yourself. The Lord does call people into things. The Lord does use things. The Lord does provide the things. The Lord does arrange the things, which in actual fact are not in His thought and mind whatsoever or at all. However, He will use them and bless them and take care of them in that realm, but you don't try to settle that up either. In the Land, you will find the Lord has pulverised it, absolutely pulverised it, and He will pulverise you too because, you see, you have got to observe an order.

Oh, if we could only learn this wonderful lesson of the book of Esther. It is the end of a dispensation. God's last word is the book of Esther. *We* are at the end of a dispensation. We are the people of God. The people of God at the end of *this* dispensation are found in two clearly distinct realms. One is the realm of Christendom and the other is what we call the Church realm. How God deals with us in one is entirely different to how He deals with us in the other. What He blesses, uses, and takes up in one He will not touch, but rather will judge and remove in the other, strangely enough. That is the explanation. Go now and read and study this book alongside the books of Ezra and Nehemiah and see whether these things are true.

10.
Esther Study Guide

The book of Esther is one of the only two books of the Bible that bear the name of a woman. As we read it, we are immediately arrested by its direct and vital style, as also by the difference of its atmosphere when compared with the other books of the Old Testament. It is thoroughly Gentile in atmosphere, customs, and even phraseology, almost to the point where it appears to shun the things of God. It is this aspect which caused its inclusion in the canon of the Old Testament to be hotly questioned and cause occasional controversy and discussion.

On the other hand, the book of Esther has always been given an esteem which is truly remarkable. It was commonly believed in Jewish circles that in the days of the Messiah only the Law and the book of Esther would remain. We ought also to note that the feast of Purim, which commemorates this event, has always been meticulously observed by the Jew from that day to this.

In the Hebrew Scriptures, Esther is found in the third division, called the writings (ketuvim), in a section called "The Five Rolls," of which it was the principal book. It is instructive to note that under the sovereignty of the Holy Spirit this book was moved to its present position as the final word of Old Testament history.

In Ezra/Nehemiah we have seen God's ways with those who returned, but what was the Lord's attitude to the great majority who remained comfortably in exile and how did He deal with them? In the book of Esther we discover the answer to our question. Twenty three chapters (Ezra and Nehemiah) deal with the remnant that returned, and ten chapters (Esther) deal with the vast majority who remained. Esther is a great corrective, on the one hand, to the narrow prejudice and dogmatism which "restrict" God to one's own realm of work and understanding, and on the other hand, to that sentimental looseness and insensitive non-discernment which would involve itself in anything that is "being blessed," as if that in itself was the criterion of God's full committal of Himself to it.

Authorship and Date

We have nothing internal or external that would give us a clue as to the authorship of Esther but whoever wrote it was minutely familiar with Persian customs and life, and obviously lived in Persia. This can also be seen from his use of terms.

From earliest times Mordecai has been suggested as the author and in all probability there is much of his work in this book. The Talmud attributes it to Ezra and the great synagogue. Nehemiah has also been suggested. The book is much more Persian than Jewish, and there can be little doubt that the present record is based on Persian documents from the royal archives (see Esther 10:2). This could argue in favour of Mordecai's authorship.

The date of the story can be fixed with some certainty between the sixth and seventh chapter of Ezra (i.e. in the 60–70 years between the first and second stage of the return from Babylon to Jerusalem), in the reign of the famous Xerxes (486–465 BC), or Ahasuerus as he is called in the book of Esther. "Ahasuerus" is probably the Hebrew transliteration of a Persian title and not a name.

The book commences with the third year of his reign (483 BC), and progresses to his marriage to Esther four years later in the seventh year of his reign (479 BC). Five years after that, in the 12th year of his reign (474 BC), Haman hatched the plot, which lies at the heart of the record (see Esther 1:3; 2:16; 3:7). Thus this book covers a period of approximately ten years.

There is little indication of the actual date of compilation, but the language used suggests that it was compiled some time after the events described. On the other hand, there is much detail that would suggest a contemporary compilation, and, furthermore, the style has a real similarity to that of Chronicles, Ezra and Nehemiah, even though thoroughly Gentile. It could be substantially therefore the work of Ezra based on a document compiled by Mordecai.

Especial Note: The Background of Esther

Xerxes, or Ahasuerus, was one of the greatest of the Persian kings. He was proudly self-willed, amorous, and given to terrible moods. His empire extended from India to Ethiopia and to the borders of Greece, including the Mediterranean Isles. He reigned from 486–465 BC.

It has never been clearly established whether Esther, (or indeed Vashti) was "the Queen", or "a Queen", because Ahasuerus had a number of wives, and many concubines. Vashti is known to us from history as a cruel and profligate woman.

We also know from history, that in the 3rd year of his reign (483 BC), Ahasuerus engaged in a disastrous campaign against Greece and in 480 BC first lost his fleet at Salamis, and later saw his army badly crippled at Thermopylae. It was after this defeat that he returned home in the 7th year of his reign (479 BC), and busied himself with matrimonial matters.

The story we have in Esther took place at Shushan (or Susa), one of the three capitals of the empires. A general conference was held there in the third year of Xerxes' reign, when the Greek expedition was planned. It was during this conference that the incident took place, which was to have such unhappy consequences for Vashti.

In Persian inscriptions the great feast, as recorded in the first chapter of Esther, is described as being preparatory to the expedition against Greece. This expedition is also described as comprising an army numbering two and a half million.

As near as can be stated, Esther became Queen in 478 BC, and the suggested date for the deliverance from the massacre is 473 BC.

The Key to the Book

The word "God", the name of God–*YHWH*, the promised land, the city of God–Jerusalem, the house of God, the law of God, the commands of God, even the Word of God, are not mentioned in Esther!! In fact, the LXX scholars in their translation of this book were so embarrassed by this lack that they elaborated on the Hebrew text to make up for it. In marked contrast, the Persian King is mentioned 192 times, his kingdom 26 times and his personal name, or title, 29 times.

Mark also the amazing difference between Ezra-Nehemiah and Esther:

In Ezra/Nehemiah	In Esther
The City of God	Sushan, a Gentile capital
The Lord	A Gentile king
The Word taught carefully	The Word of God not mentioned
The law of God observed	The law of God not mentioned
All worship	No worship
Separation for witness	Esther not known as a Jewess
Mixed marriage condemned	A mixed marriage not condemned

Furthermore, we must add to this the fact that the name Esther was foreign, and not a Hebrew name, corresponding to 'Venus', and implying 'good luck'. Esther's Hebrew name was 'Hadassah' which means 'myrtle'. (Esther 2:7)

In all Jewish homes of the dispersion, idolatry was forbidden, and the law of God was respected, if not understood. Yet the Jews described in Esther remained where God's purpose could not be realized, God's house could not be built and God's Messiah could not be born.

It is in this atmosphere that the story of Esther takes place. Everywhere we discover the hidden sovereignty of God working for His people. And working for them in spite of their location, their ignorance, their compromise, their lack of devotion and zeal.

It is most clearly seen in the hidden manner in which the name of God appears in Esther. Four times and always at points of crisis in the story, the name "Jehovah", appears in Hebrew in acrostic form (Esther 1:20; 5:4; 5:13; 7:9). In the first two instances, it is initial letters; in the last two instances it is spelled backwards; in the second and fourth, it is spelled forwards. This evidently can be no coincidence! Beyond these four instances, the name of the Lord "I AM that I AM", appears in Hebrew once, also in acrostics (Esther 7:5). See Chart I. Note that where initial letters are used, the facts are final; where they are spelled backwards, it is God's overruling, and where forwards, it is God's direct working.

What does all this teach us? It reveals the sovereign grace of God toward all those who are His own wherever they may be found and this lesson is illustrated in Esther by the remarkable deliverance, and the honour and joy which followed it. The lesson appears to be that God would not build His temple in Babylon, or Shushan; He would not dwell among them, but He was for them. We need to recognize, therefore, that at that time the people of God were to be found in two realms, the exile or the land, and though the saving grace of God was the same toward all of His own in whichever realm they lived, the principles upon which He dealt with them were different.

In the first realm, the exile, it was all acts, blessings, things, experiences. It was all real, wonderful and practical but it was not the 'building of His house and city'. It knew of the Lord as Saviour, deliverer, healer and provider, but it was in Shushan or Babylon, exiled from the land. It was a real knowing of the Lord but in a place where both His house and home could not be built, or His purpose concerning the coming of the Messiah be fulfilled. They knew God visiting them, saving them, blessing them, delivering them but not making His home among them.

It is in the second realm, the land that we come to the heart of the matter. For if the prophetic promise of the Messiah's coming was to be fulfilled, then the house of God and Jerusalem had to be rebuilt, the land repopulated, Bethlehem rebuilt, and Galilee restored etc. (see e.g. Isaiah 9:1, 6; Micah 5:2–4).

Esther, Mordecai, and the Jews in exile could have lived, or died, but it would have made no difference to God's purpose concerning the coming of the Messiah. For even if there had been no deliverance of the Jews in exile, it would not have adversely affected the fulfillment of God's program. That was dependent upon those who had returned to the land.

We see then that Zerubbabel, Ezra, Nehemiah and the remnant who returned to the land, at great sacrifice, were a vital and integral part of God's purpose concerning the coming of the Messiah. Through them He fulfilled His prophetic word and realized His purpose.

The key to the book of Esther is the truth that God never leaves or forsakes His own. His sovereign grace and love is there working for them wherever they may be found, blessing them, using them, and delivering them.

Here we learn a vital lesson for our own time at the end of the age. There are two realms in which God's people are found. We are either found spiritually in that area where the Church of God, the house of God cannot be built, or in that area where it can. No matter where we are found God never forsakes His redeemed children but in His grace he blesses them, provides for them, and works miracles for them although He may not be treating them as 'living stones,' which He is building into a spiritual house for His eternal dwelling place.

The Outline of the Book

We can see in Esther a threefold division:

I. The sovereignty of God determining the matter before the event or crisis. Esther 1:1—2:23

II. The event or crisis itself. Esther 3:1—5:8

III. God sovereignly intervening in deliverance and turning the evil into honour and glory. Esther 5:9—10:3

We need to keep continually before us all that has been said about the background of this book and the fact that in this realm God in his grace works sovereignly in a veiled way.

I. The sovereignty of God determining the matter before the event or crisis. Esther 1:1—2:23

A. The story

1. The great conference 1:1—8

All the civil an d military leaders were invited. It was a display at the Persian court of amazing wealth and luxury. There were two feasts, one at the beginning of the conference, and one at the end.

2. The royal command to Vashti 1:9–12

It was during the final feast that Vashti was asked to come before the assembled leaders. Her refusal was a public affront to the King and caused great anger.

3. The divorce and deposition of Vashti 1:13–22

The divorce of Vashti was by royal decree and was recorded in the state and royal accounts

4. Esther chosen as Queen 2:1–18

By royal decree the replacement of Vashti was to be found through an empire-wide beauty competition. Esther is now introduced in the story, and she was known for her great beauty. Mordecai was her cousin (2:7). According to Jewish tradition she was born of the line of King Saul (2:5) and of Shimei (See II Samuel 16:5, 6); her father died just before she was born and her mother during her birth. She was favoured by the chief officer of the Harem and advanced before the other competitors. Note Mordecai's advice to keep her Jewish identity a secret. Esther chosen as Queen.

5. Mordecai's discovery of a plot 2:19–23

Mordecai's discovery of a plot to assassinate the king, and Esther's timely intervention which saved the king's life brought about a good relationship to the King.

B. The lessons

1. The sovereignty of God behind the scenes

The scene may be one of absolute and autocratic world power and authority but God is there in a hidden way and is absolute Lord of all. Long before the events described, He has planned His counteraction and His deliverance. Note Vashti's deposition; Mordecai's connection with the court; Esther's selection as queen; Mordecai's overhearing of the plot to assassinate the King. There is in fact no situation beyond the authority of the Lord. All is foreseen by Him and action is taken by Him accordingly.

2. The sovereign grace of God in caring for His own

In spite of the compromised condition of His people, and their 'comfortable' lethargy, in His grace and love He plans their deliverance and their triumph. He arranges and uses circumstances, and takes hold of the conditions as they are in order to deliver His people, simply because they are His own. He does things in the exile which He would not touch in the holy land. For example, in the exile He arranges the marriage of Esther to a heathen and unsaved king, yet in the land, He teaches His own through Ezra to divorce their foreign and unbelieving wives.

II. The event itself – the annihilation of God's people planned and timed. Esther 3:1–5:8

A. The Story

1. Haman the Agagite 3:1–6

Haman's greatness and Mordecai's attitude to Him. The obeisance demanded by Haman was probably of religious significance (3:2 cp v.4). Haman's anger and its resulting genocide planned.

2. The plot to destroy the Jews 3:7–15

The lots cast and the date of the planned massacre settled. This was done according to astrology. These lots – 'pur' or 'purim' in Hebrew – are the origination of the name of the festival 'Purim' The king approached; his assent given and the royal decree made. Is it not interesting that Haman was descended from Agag and Mordecai from Kish and Saul (3:1, cp. 1 Samuel 15)? We know that Saul did not obey the Lord's command to destroy all the Amalekites and some of Agag's seed survived. By the grace of God Mordecai triumphed where Saul failed.

3. The reaction of Esther, Mordecai and the Jews 4:1—5:8

Mordecai's anguish; the Jews' fasting; Esther's concern; Mordecai's counsel; Esther's courage; the three days fast; Esther's "success."

B. The lessons

1. Satan's bitter hatred of all God's people

This bitter hatred of Satan for all of God's people continues even when they are not where they should be, when they are compromised or backsliding. His antagonism toward them is so deeply entrenched that he will always seek to destroy them because of their relationship to Christ. His plans are always carefully laid and timed and are never haphazard

2. The Anguish and Intercession of God's People.

His people sought His face with sincerity and urgency. It is a noteworthy fact that the Lord always allows His people to be reduced to "crying to Him" before He delivers them. (See Psalm 107). God had carefully prepared their deliverance, and yet He still awaited their cry! We must also note the sad fact that their anguish was not so much over the Lord's name, and honour, and purpose, as over their own i.e. their preservation. "I" and, "we", so often characterises that realm.

3. The Sovereign Grace of God

In His Sovereign Grace He has those who at such a time are faithful, prepared and ready.

God sovereignly intervening in deliverance and turning the Evil into honour and glory (5:9–10:3)

A. The Story

1. The King Honours Mordecai (5:9–6:14)

Haman's design; the king's sleeplessness and the result; Haman's humiliation

2. Esther's petition granted (7:1–10)

A second feast; Esther's petition to the king; his wrath concerning Haman; the execution of Haman

3. The king's former decree counteracted (8:1–17)

A Persian Royal decree was unalterable; Esther's fears; the making of a new decree; Haman's house and property confiscated; Mordecai's position.

4. The day of destruction turned into the day of triumph (9:1–16)

The 13th day of the 12th month.

5. The Feast of Purim instituted (9:17–32)

The 14th and 15th day of the 12th month set aside for all time for the commemoration of the great deliverance of the Jewish people. This is the feast of Purim commemorated to this day wherever Jews are found.

6. The Honours, Greatness and Prosperity of Mordecai and the Jews (10:1–3)

The end of the matter- Mordecai and the Jews given much honour and respect, and prosper greatly. What had been meant for their destruction turned into their advancement and honour.

B. The Lessons

1. God in His Sovereignty knows the exact point at which to intervene. He "arranged" the king's sleeplessness and the resulting deliverance of the Jews. It is comforting to know that He who keeps Israel neither slumbers nor sleeps. He knows the exact time when to intervene, and who to use.

2. It is instructive to note the remarkable and delicate balance between God's sovereign working and man's cooperation–Esther, Mordecai.

3. The way in which God always takes the very things that caused the trouble, to work deliverance. Haman unwittingly plan's Mordecai's honours; Haman builds the gallows–He and his sons are hanged on them: the Royal decree was intended for destruction, but the Royal Decree brought preservation. The day of destruction became the day of deliverance and the enemies' destruction.

4. The very things that caused the trouble are the means God uses to honour, prosper and increase His own

5. We learn from all this that it is possible to have real experience of the Lord, His deliverance, blessing, provision, etc. in that realm.

6. We learn, too, that in His sovereign grace, He makes His own to be great, influential, and prosperous in that realm.

7. Yet we also learn that it had no real bearing upon the Purpose of God, and the coming of the Messiah. It is therefore possible to be blessed, used, etc., and not be within God's eternal purpose.

The Message of the Book

The book of Esther is truly amazing, for what all that precedes has been at such pains to teach us, it contradicts! And indeed, more merely than contradicts, for here in this book, the very contradictions are blessed and used of God!!

To get down to the reason for this, is not only to understand the vital message of Esther, but to also understand the seemingly contradictory and complex situation today.

Esther reveals to us that there are two distinct realms in which God's people are found - "The Land" and "The Exile". The minority have returned to the Land and the majority have remained in the Exile. The way the Lord deals with His people in these two realms is entirely different. For what in one He would never touch, but rather judge and remove, in the other He will bless and even use! He might even arrange it!!! We can never, therefore, make what He touches, blesses or uses in "the Exile", the criterion for "the Land".

Today we are also at the end of a dispensation. We also have the two realms in which God's people are found; therefore we need to understand clearly the message of Esther.

With this book, we have come to the end of the second section of the Old Testament, the historical books. It is then highly instructive, that whilst there would be the so called 400 silent years before the age was concluded, the Lord's last word as far as divinely recorded history is concerned, was to do with the majority of His people who remain where His Purpose can never be realized. And it is a glorious declaration of the grace of God toward all who are His wherever they may be found and in whatever condition!

The Name of God in the Book of Esther

יהוה Jehovah
see letters with underlines in Hebrew in examples following

i. Esther 1:20
Initial letters; backwards.
(note Hebrew is written right to left)

הֶיא וְכָל־הַנשים יִתְּנוּ

Pronunciation (read from left to right):
hî wə·k̲āl han·nā·šîm yit·tə·nū

Literally:

הֶיא	She (Strong's # H1931)
וְכָל־	and all (Strong's # H3605)
הַנשים	the wives (Strong's # H802)
יִתְּנוּ	will owe (Strong's H5414)

An example in English:
Due **R**espect **O**ur **L**adies all
Shall give their husbands, great and small.

ii. Esther 5:4

Initial letters; forwards.

Hebrew: read right to left

יָבוֹא הַמֶּלֶךְ וְהָמָן הַיּוֹם

Pronunciation (read from left to right):
yā·ḇō·w ham·me·lek̲ wə·hā·mān hay·yō·wm

Literally:	יָבוֹא	*will come*	*(Strong's # H935)*
	הַמֶּלֶךְ	*the king*	*(Strong's # H4428)*
	וְהָמָן	*and Haman*	*(Strong's # H2001)*
	הַיּוֹם	*today*	*(Strong's # H3117)*

An example in English:
Let **O**ur **R**oyal **D**inner bring
Haman feasting with a King

iii. Esther 5:13
Final letters; backwards
Hebrew: read right to left

זֶה אֵינֶנּוּ שׁוֶה לִי

Pronunciation (read from left to right):
zeh ʾê·nen·nū šō·weh lî

Literally: זֶה   *this*   *(Strong's # H2088)*

אֵינֶנּוּ   *nothing (Strong's # H369)*

שׁוֶה   *avail (Strong's # H7737)*

לִי   *to me*   *(no Strong's #. A preposition)*

An example in English:
Grand for no avail my state
While this Jew sits at the gate.

iv. Esther 7:7
Final letters; forwards
Hebrew: read right to left

כִּי־כָלְתָה אֵלָיו הָרָעָה

Pronunciation (read from left to right):
kî-kā·lə·ṯāh 'ê·lāw hā·rā·'āh

Literally:	כִּי	*that*	*(Strong's # H3588)*
	כָלְתָה	*determined*	*(Strong's # H3615)*
	אֵלָיו	*against*	*(Strong's # H413)*
	הָרָעָה	*evil*	*(Strong's # H7451)*

An example in English:
*I**ll** **t**o fear decree**d** I find,*
Toward me in the monarch's mind

Note that in these four instances it is the Name of the Lord—
Jehovah, or Yahweh (YHWH).

v. Esther 7:5

אהיה I AM

Final letter, forward.
Hebrew: read right to left

הוּא זֶה וְאֵי־זֶה

Pronunciation (read from left to right):
hū zeh wə·'ê-zeh

Literally: הוּא   *he*   (Strong's # H1931)
              זֶה   *this one* (Strong's # H2088)
              וְאֵי   *whence*   (Strong's # H335)
              זֶה   *this one* (Strong's # H2088)

An example in English:
*Wher**e** dwellet**h** the Enem**y** that daret**h***
presume in his heart to do this thing

Note that in this instance it is the name 'I AM that I AM'; (EHYH)
(All this from E.W. Bullinger and A.T. Pierson)

Questions

1. What does the name "Esther" mean?

2. What period of history is covered by the book of Esther, and into which part of the book of Ezra can it be fitted?

3. Write three or four sentences on each of the following:
a) Vashti

b) Haman

c) Ahasuerus

d) Shushan (or Susan)

4. Write an account of the feasts, banquets, and conferences which are found in the book of Esther, stating their importance.

5. Show five ways in which the name of God appears in Esther. Give Scripture references:

1.

2.

3.

4.

5.

6. How vital were the people of God who remained in Babylon, to the practical realization of God's eternal purpose, and to the bringing in of the Messiah. Give reasons for your answer.

7. State in your own words, what is the message of the book of Esther. Is it possible for Christians to be in "the land" or in "the exile: today?

8. Describe how God takes Satan's plans to destroy God's people, and uses these evil plans, to bring joy and even greater security to the people of God. Does this teach you anything about the way the Lord deals with Satan in world history, throughout all ages?

9. Do you find anything puzzling about God's dealing with His people in Esther, as compared with His dealings with His people in Ezra/Nehemiah? What lesson, if any, do you learn from this comparison?

10. Describe briefly the part played by Mordecai in the Book of Esther. What do you most admire about Esther herself, in this book?

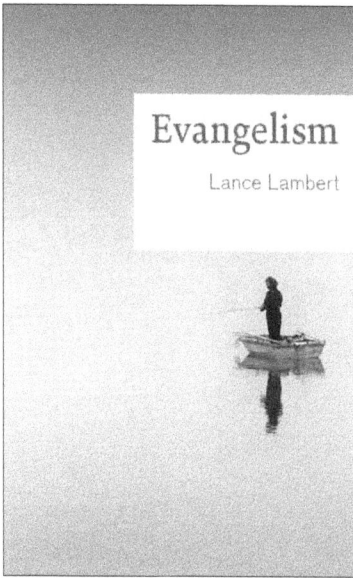

Evangelism

What is God's purpose in evangelism?

It is clear that the Word of God commands us to preach the gospel to every creature, to go into the whole world and make disciples of all nations baptising them in the name of the Father, the Son and the Holy Spirit.

So how do we do it?

In "Evangelism" Lance opens the scriptures to reveal how the church can practically and effectively preach the gospel to the unsaved world, by revealing to them in scripture their need for a Saviour, the work of the Saviour, and how to receive the Saviour. He explains practical means of winning souls and how to follow-up with the newly saved to make disciples of the Lord Jesus. Evangelism is the way by which we gather the materials for the house of God.

So faith comes by hearing, and hearing through the word of Christ.

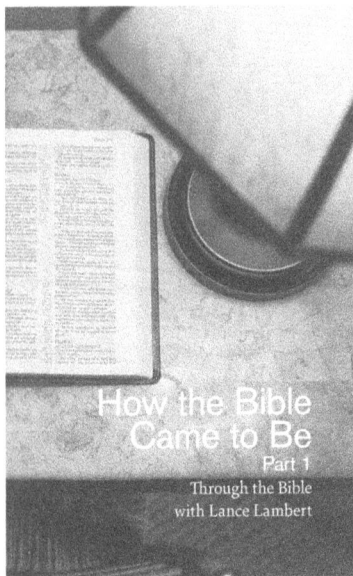

How the Bible Came to Be: Part 1

How is the Bible still as applicable in the 21st century as it was when it was first penned? How did so many authors, with different backgrounds and over thousands of years, write something so perfectly fitting with one another?

Lance Lambert breaks down these, and many other questions in this first volume of his series teaching through the Bible. He lays a firm foundation for going on to study the Word of the living God.

And ye shall seek me, and find me, when ye shall search for me with all your heart.
Jeremiah 29:13

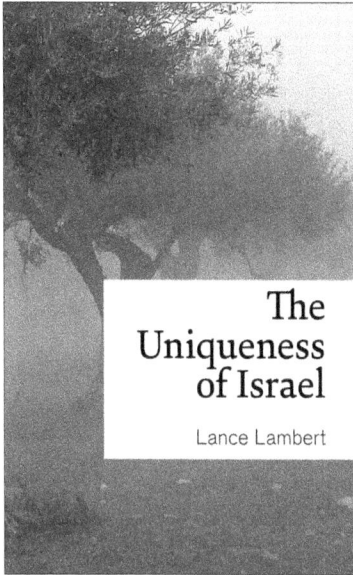

The Uniqueness of Israel

Woven into the fabric of Jewish existence there is an undeniable uniqueness. There is bitter controversy over the subject of Israel, but time itself will establish the truth about this nation's place in God's plan. For Lance Lambert, the Lord Jesus is the key that unlocks Jewish history He is the key not only to their fall, but also to their restoration. For in spite of the fact that they rejected Him, He has not rejected them.

Fellowship
Lance Lambert

Fellowship

Ephesians 2 says that we are in the household of God are to be built up together for a habitation for God in the Spirit.

What does this mean for you and me to be built up together with other believers? How should we contribute to the building work of Christ? What are the principles that govern this fellowship and building work?

In this current volume, Lance Lambert addresses these and other questions. He shares how "God has always desired a dwelling place in which He can express Himself, reveal Himself and manifest Himself, as it were, a place in which He can find His home."

Thank the Lord this is His heart's desire—to be with us and let us know Him. How blessed we are!